CEFR **A1+**

Base Camp

Live Escalate

Teruhiko Kadoyama
Live ABC editors

Book **1**

 *SEIBIDO* **LiveABC**

photographs

iStockphoto

StreamLine

Web 動画・音声ファイルのストリーミング再生について

CD マーク及び Web 動画マークがある箇所は、PC、スマートフォン、タブレット端末において、無料でストリーミング再生することができます。下記 URL よりご利用ください。再生手順や動作環境などは本書巻末の「Web 動画のご案内」をご覧ください。

http://st.seibido.co.jp

音声ファイルのダウンロードについて

CD マークがある箇所は、ダウンロードすることも可能です。下記 URL の書籍詳細ページにあるダウンロードアイコンをクリックしてください。

http://seibido.co.jp/ad594

Live Escalate Book 1: Base Camp

Contents

CONTENT CHART

UNIT	COMMUNICATION STRATEGY	VOCABULARY
UNIT 01 Meeting New People	• Talking about where people are from • Introducing different greetings from around the world	• Greetings • Physical appearance • Nationalities
UNIT 02 School Life	• Exchanging personal information • Introducing how a flipped classroom is different from a traditional classroom	• Majors • Zodiac signs • School clubs
UNIT 03 Seeing a Doctor	• Describing symptoms of illnesses	• Body parts • Health problems
UNIT 04 Expressing Yourself	• Expressing feelings and emotions • Introducing a psychology test about colors	• Adjectives of feelings and emotions
UNIT 05 Getting Around	• Describing modes of transportation • Discussing how we should use priority seats	• Types of transportation
UNIT 06 Talking about the Time	• Practicing having telephone conversations	• The 12 months of the year • Dates
REVIEW 1 Review 1		
UNIT 07 Eating Out	• Practicing how to order a meal in a restaurant • Talking about different restaurants	• Food and drinks • Utensils • Adjectives describing food
UNIT 08 At the Supermarket	• Giving directions	• Places and shops • Locations • Transportation
UNIT 09 Hobbies	• Talking about what people do in their free time	• Recreational activities • Parkour
UNIT 10 Shop Till You Drop	• Introducing clothes and accessories • Talking about the benefits of online shopping	• Clothes and accessories • Sizes and measurements
UNIT 11 Going on Vacation	• Talking about trip plans	• Trip plans
UNIT 12 Sports	• Talking about one's favorite sports	• Types of sports
REVIEW 2 Review 2		

CONVERSATION	GRAMMAR	READING
Where Do You Come From?	• Present Simple—Be Verbs • Present Simple—Base Verbs	How Do You Shake Hands?
What's Your Zodiac Sign?	• Wh- Questions • Present Continuous	Flipped Classroom
What's the Matter?	• Past Simple—Be Verbs • Past Simple—Base Verbs	Patient Information Form
How Was Last Weekend?	• Tense Comparison	What "Color" Are You?
The World Traveler	• Infinitives and Gerunds • Transportation Preposition	How We Should Use Priority Seats
What Were You Doing?	• Past Continuous • Past Continuous + When + Past Simple	Summer Camp Schedule
What'll You Have?	• Future Tense • Be Going To	A World of Restaurants
Getting Everything on the List	• Modal Verbs • Countable / Uncountable Nouns	Huge Discounts This Week Only!
Exploring New Hobbies	• Linking Verbs • Possessive Pronouns	Parkour: The Art of Movement
Finding the Right Fit	• Passive Voice • Verbs Related to Time and Money	Online Shopping Catches On
Making a Last-Minute Booking	• Quantity Pronouns • Indefinite Pronouns	Italy's Beautiful Secret: The Blue Grotto
What Sports Do You Like?	• Comparative and Superlative Adjectives	Challenge Yourself in the Ironman Triathlon

LEARNING OVERVIEW

The Live Escalate series comes in three volumes, from Book 1: Base Camp to Book 3: Summit. Each book is made up of 12 units and a review section after every six units. The following is the introduction for Book 1: Base Camp. There are reading, listening, writing, and speaking activities in each unit. Readers will be challenged by the variety of fun and interesting content throughout the series.

WARM UP

A warm-up section of the theme topic

Students learn the vocabulary words and sentences through visual input and listening.

Students practice speaking skills by role-playing with partners. After that, they listen to a short talk related to the theme topic to finish the warm-up section.

CONVERSATION

A dialogue about the theme topic with a variety of questions

The dialogues use realistic, modern English to deliver practical and fun conversation practice.

Here, students will find various types of activities that will assess their understanding. Completing these tasks will help students feel confident in their English ability.

GRAMMAR

Explicit and lively grammar instruction through visuals

Students' grammar ability is tested through a variety of exercise types.

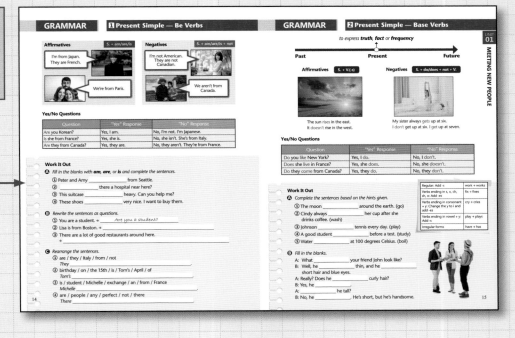

READING

An article about the theme topic with a variety of questions

The article features compelling topics and is filled with fascinating facts and information.

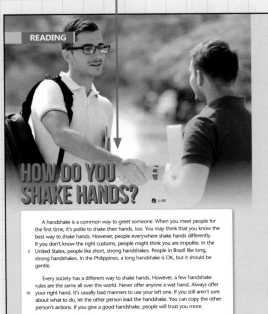

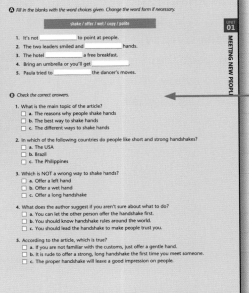

Students will check their comprehension with different types of review questions.

LEARNING OVERVIEW

WRITING

Ⓐ Look at the picture and answer the questions below.

INTERNATIONAL PASSPORT

PASSPORT	TYPE	CODE OF	PASSPORT NO.
PASSPORT	P	ISSUING STATE	AA 012345678
		WWW	

SURNAME
DOE
GIVEN NAMES
JANE
NATIONALITY
British
DATE OF BIRTH
30 10 1988
SEX
F
PLACE OF BIRTH   AUTHORITY
London
DATE OF ISSUE   HOLDERS SIGNATURE
DATE OF EXPIRY   *JaneDoe*

① What's the woman's last name?

② Where does the woman come from?

③ Is her birthday on September 30?

④ Does the woman have long hair?

⑤ What's her passport number?

Ⓑ Rewrite the following sentences as negative sentences and questions.

① Sarah has a laptop.
  Sarah doesn't have a laptop.   *Does Sarah have a laptop?*

② Emma comes from Boston.

③ Handshake rules are the same around the world.

④ Josh often plays basketball.

⑤ Henry and Bob know a lot about computers.

18

WRITING

Practice sentence patterns that use the theme topic and grammar points

This section presents students with real-life writing tasks, such as letters and menus. Students will improve their writing skills while having fun along the way!

CHALLENGE YOURSELF

A topic-related listening test

This section provides an excellent tool for students to track their improvement and be aware of the improvement in their English proficiency.

CHALLENGE YOURSELF

Part I Pictures   🎧 1-06

Look at the picture and choose the best answer.

1.

☐ a   ☐ b   ☐ c

2.

☐ a   ☐ b   ☐ c

Part II Question & Response   🎧 1-07

Listen to the statement or question and choose the best response.

3. ☐ a   ☐ b   ☐ c   5. ☐ a   ☐ b   ☐ c
4. ☐ a   ☐ b   ☐ c   6. ☐ a   ☐ b   ☐ c

Part III Conversations   🎧 1-08

Listen to the conversation and answer the questions.

7. Where does the second speaker
   come from?
   ☐ a. She comes from Hong Kong.
   ☐ b. She comes from Japan.
   ☐ c. She comes from the United
        States.

8. What are the speakers talking about?
   ☐ a. Their new teacher
   ☐ b. Their classmate
   ☐ c. Their homework

9. What is true?
   ☐ a. They're old friends.
   ☐ b. He called her yesterday.
   ☐ c. They're new friends.

10. Why is Tom not there?
    ☐ a. He lives somewhere new.
    ☐ b. He got sick.
    ☐ c. He's in trouble.

Linguaporta Training

Let's review the unit with Linguaporta.

19

WELCOME TO *LIVE ESCALATE*!

The Live Escalate series comes in three volumes, from Book 1: Base Camp to Book 3: Summit. Each book is made up of 12 units and a review section after every six units. There are reading, listening, writing, and speaking activities in each unit. Readers will be challenged by the variety of fun and interesting content throughout the series.

A Complete Series

Each of the three books in this stimulating and pragmatic series is designed with a natural flow in mind: listening ⇨ speaking ⇨ reading ⇨ writing, with the result being that your English improves dramatically while you're unaware of the effort you've spent. The aim is that with minimal friction, learners of all ages will assimilate this language with the same fluidity a child does in his or her native environment, thus removing the sense of foreign-ness and frustration that is part of foreign language learning.

Unit Themes Focusing on Self-Expression

The units covered in this series pertain to ordinary life, focusing on the types of situations and challenges learners encounter every day, including shopping, eating, socializing, odds and ends around the house, leisure, and more.

Book 3: Summit
I CAN express opinions on some matters in a controlled way.

Book 2: Trekking
I CAN express opinions in a controlled way.

Book 1: Base Camp
I CAN take part in a conversation on a familiar topic.

WARM UP

A *Listen to the short conversations. Each conversation is about greetings and introductions. Write the numbers in the correct boxes and the sentences in the blanks.* 🔊 1-02

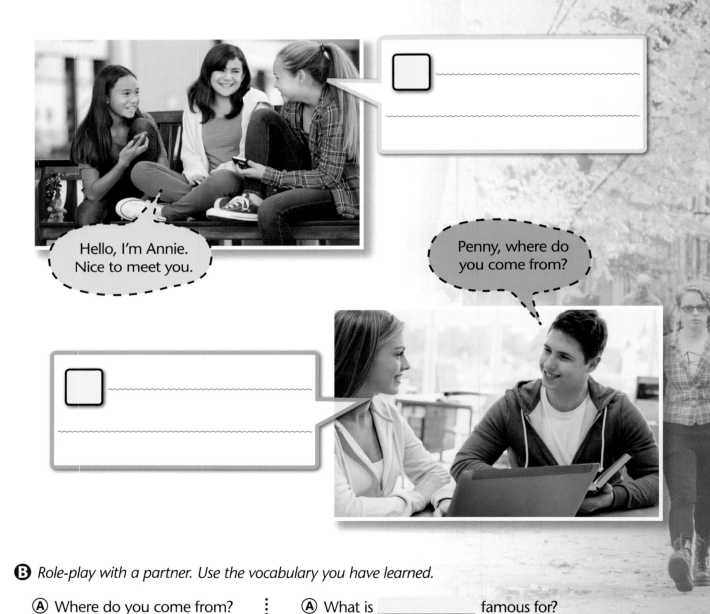

Hello, I'm Annie. Nice to meet you.

Penny, where do you come from?

B *Role-play with a partner. Use the vocabulary you have learned.*

Ⓐ Where do you come from?

Ⓑ I come from _____.

Ⓐ What is _____ famous for?

Ⓑ It's famous for _____.

Penny, this is Joe. Joe, this is Penny.

It's famous for pasta.

No, I come from Australia.

Where Do You Come From?

A *Watch the video clip and check the correct answers.* WEB動画 💻

1. Where is Mark from?
   - ☐ **a.** New York
   - ☐ **b.** Boston
   - ☐ **c.** Canada

2. How does Heidi feel about the city?
   - ☐ **a.** She knows a lot about it.
   - ☐ **b.** It's new to her.
   - ☐ **c.** She doesn't like it here.

3. What is Boston famous for?
   - ☐ **a.** Bread
   - ☐ **b.** Fish
   - ☐ **c.** Pasta

4. Who is Karen?
   - ☐ **a.** Their teacher
   - ☐ **b.** Their parent
   - ☐ **c.** Their class leader

B *Listen to the conversation and fill in the blanks.* 🎧 1-03 💻

Heidi is a new student. Mark is showing her their college.

Mark: Hello, Heidi. I'm Mark. Nice to meet you.

Heidi: Nice to meet you, too.

Mark: How do you ¹_____ about here?

Heidi: I don't ²_____ this city at all. It's very new to me.

Mark: Where do you come from?

Heidi: I come from New York. I ³_____ up there.

Mark: I love New York. I think it's a great city.

Heidi: Do you come from New York, too?

Mark: No. I come from ⁴_____, but I went to New York in 2015. I really ⁵_____ it.

Heidi: Boston is famous for ⁶_____, right?

Mark: Yes. All of our fish is great.

Heidi notices Karen.

Heidi: Who's that pretty girl?

Mark: She is our class ⁷_____. Her name is Karen.

Heidi: She is so ⁸_____ and thin.

Mark: Yes, let's go say hello to her!

C *Practice the conversation with your partner.*

D *Listen to the three short conversations. Where are they from? Number the pictures 1 to 3 and check the details about them.* 🎧 1-04

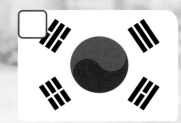

☐ short   ☐ black hair   ☐ tall   ☐ strong   ☐ chubby   ☐ curly hair
☐ long hair   ☐ brown eyes   ☐ thin   ☐ green eyes   ☐ short hair   ☐ blue eyes

GRAMMAR   **1 Present Simple — Be Verbs**

Affirmatives   `S. + am/are/is`

I'm from Japan.
They are French.

We're from Paris.

Negatives   `S. + am/are/is + not`

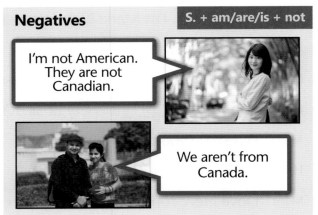

I'm not American.
They are not
Canadian.

We aren't from
Canada.

Yes/No Questions

Question	"Yes" Response	"No" Response
Are you Korean?	Yes, I am.	No, I'm not. I'm Japanese.
Is she from France?	Yes, she is.	No, she isn't. She's from Italy.
Are they from Canada?	Yes, they are.	No, they aren't. They're from France.

Work It Out

A *Fill in the blanks with **am**, **are**, or **is** and complete the sentences.*

① Peter and Amy _____ from Seattle.

② _____ there a hospital near here?

③ This suitcase _____ heavy. Can you help me?

④ These shoes _____ very nice. I want to buy them.

B *Rewrite the sentences as questions.*

① You are a student. ➔ _____ *Are you a student?* _____

② Lisa is from Boston. ➔ _____

③ There are a lot of good restaurants around here.
➔ _____

C *Rearrange the sentences.*

① are / they / Italy / from / not
They _____.

② birthday / on / the 15th / is / Tom's / April / of
Tom's _____.

③ is / student / Michelle / exchange / an / from / France
Michelle _____.

④ are / people / any / perfect / not / there
There _____.

14

GRAMMAR ② Present Simple — Base Verbs

*to express **truth**, **fact** or **frequency***

Past → Present → Future

Affirmatives S. + V.(-s)

The sun rises in the east.
It doesn't rise in the west.

Negatives S. + do/does + not + V.

My sister always gets up at six.
I don't get up at six. I get up at seven.

Yes/No Questions

Question	"Yes" Response	"No" Response
Do you like New York?	Yes, I do.	No, I don't.
Does she live in France?	Yes, she does.	No, she doesn't.
Do they come from Canada?	Yes, they do.	No, they don't.

Work It Out

Regular: Add -s	work → works
Verbs ending in s, x, ch, sh, o: Add -es	fix → fixes
Verbs ending in consonant + y: Change the y to i and add -es	cry → cries
Verbs ending in vowel + y: Add -s	play → plays
Irregular forms	have → has

Ⓐ *Complete the sentences based on the hints given.*

① The moon _____ around the earth. (go)
② Cindy always _____ her cup after she drinks coffee. (wash)
③ Johnson _____ tennis every day. (play)
④ A good student _____ before a test. (study)
⑤ Water _____ at 100 degrees Celsius. (boil)

Ⓑ *Fill in the blanks.*

A: What _____ your friend John look like?
B: Well, he _____ thin, and he _____ short hair and blue eyes.
A: Really? Does he _____ curly hair?
B: Yes, he _____.
A: _____ he tall?
B: No, he _____. He's short, but he's handsome.

15

HOW DO YOU SHAKE HANDS?

🎧 1-05

A handshake is a common way to greet someone. When you meet people for the first time, it's polite to shake their hands, too. You may think that you know the best way to shake hands. However, people everywhere shake hands differently. If you don't know the right customs, people might think you are impolite. In the
5   United States, people like short, strong handshakes. People in Brazil like long, strong handshakes. In the Philippines, a long handshake is OK, but it should be gentle.

Every society has a different way to shake hands. However, a few handshake rules are the same all over the world. Never offer anyone a wet hand. Always offer
10 your right hand. It's usually bad manners to use your left one. If you still aren't sure about what to do, let the other person lead the handshake. You can copy the other person's actions. If you give a good handshake, people will trust you more.

A *Fill in the blanks with the word choices given. Change the word form if necessary.*

shake / offer / wet / copy / polite

1. It's not _____ to point at people.

2. The two leaders smiled and _____ hands.

3. The hotel _____ a free breakfast.

4. Bring an umbrella or you'll get _____.

5. Paula tried to _____ the dancer's moves.

B *Check the correct answers.*

1. What is the main topic of the article?
   - ☐ **a.** The reasons why people shake hands
   - ☐ **b.** The best way to shake hands
   - ☐ **c.** The different ways to shake hands

2. In which of the following countries do people like short and strong handshakes?
   - ☐ **a.** The USA
   - ☐ **b.** Brazil
   - ☐ **c.** The Philippines

3. Which is NOT a wrong way to shake hands?
   - ☐ **a.** Offer a left hand
   - ☐ **b.** Offer a wet hand
   - ☐ **c.** Offer a long handshake

4. What does the author suggest if you aren't sure about what to do?
   - ☐ **a.** You can let the other person offer the handshake first.
   - ☐ **b.** You should know handshake rules around the world.
   - ☐ **c.** You should lead the handshake to make people trust you.

5. According to the article, which is true?
   - ☐ **a.** If you are not familiar with the customs, just offer a gentle hand.
   - ☐ **b.** It is rude to offer a strong, long handshake the first time you meet someone.
   - ☐ **c.** The proper handshake will leave a good impression on people.

A *Look at the picture and answer the questions below.*

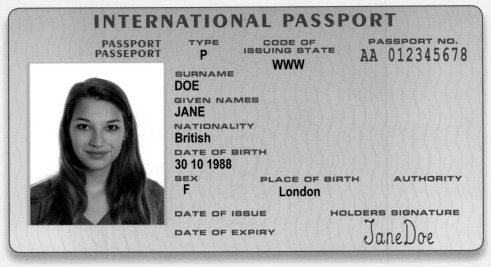

① What's the woman's last name?
_____

② Where does the woman come from?
_____

③ Is her birthday on September 30?
_____

④ Does the woman have long hair?
_____

⑤ What's her passport number?
_____

B *Rewrite the following sentences as negative sentences and questions.*

① Sarah has a laptop.
    Sarah doesn't have a laptop.   *Does Sarah have a laptop?*

② Emma comes from Boston.
_____   _____

③ Handshake rules are the same around the world.
_____   _____

④ Josh often plays basketball.
_____   _____

⑤ Henry and Bob know a lot about computers.
_____   _____

CHALLENGE YOURSELF

Look at the picture and choose the best answer.

1.

☐ a ☐ b ☐ c

2.

☐ a ☐ b ☐ c

Listen to the statement or question and choose the best response.

3. ☐ a ☐ b ☐ c   5. ☐ a ☐ b ☐ c
4. ☐ a ☐ b ☐ c   6. ☐ a ☐ b ☐ c

Listen to the conversation and answer the questions.

7. Where does the second speaker
   come from?
   ☐ a. She comes from Hong Kong.
   ☐ b. She comes from Japan.
   ☐ c. She comes from the United
       States.

8. What are the speakers talking about?
   ☐ a. Their new teacher
   ☐ b. Their classmate
   ☐ c. Their homework

9. What is true?
   ☐ a. They're old friends.
   ☐ b. He called her yesterday.
   ☐ c. They're new friends.

10. Why is Tom not there?
    ☐ a. He lives somewhere new.
    ☐ b. He got sick.
    ☐ c. He's in trouble.

Linguaporta Training

Let's review the unit with Linguaporta.

School Life

WARM UP

Ⓐ *Listen to the short conversations and match the pictures with the numbers below. Then, write the sentences in the blanks.* 🎧 1-09

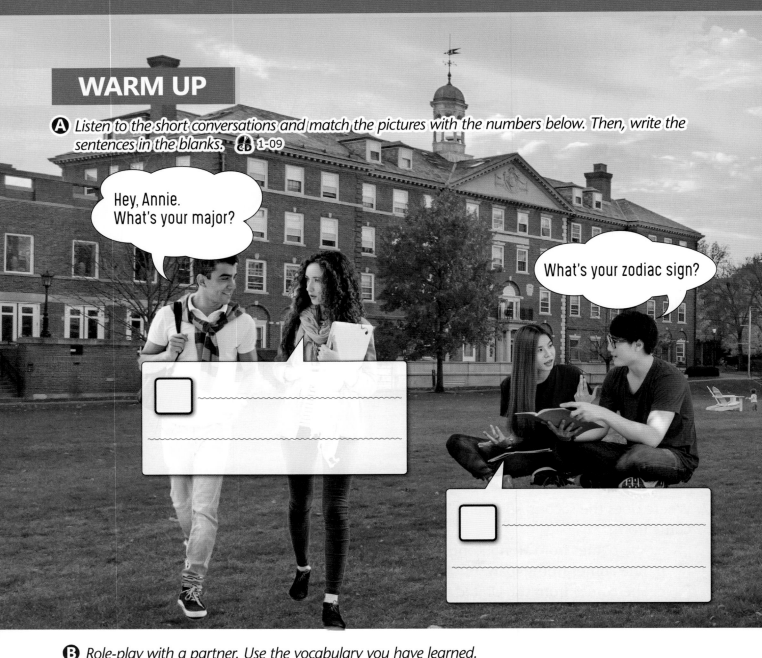

Hey, Annie.
What's your major?

What's your zodiac sign?

Ⓑ *Role-play with a partner. Use the vocabulary you have learned.*

Ⓐ What's your major?

Ⓑ My major is _____.

Ⓐ Are you in any school clubs?

Ⓑ Yes, I am. I'm in the _____. / No, I'm not

Ⓐ What's your zodiac sign?

Ⓑ I'm a(n) _____.

Ⓐ Where do you live?

Ⓑ I live _____.

Do you know your zodiac sign?

Aries (03/21-04/20)	♈	Taurus (04/21-05/21)	♉	Gemini (05/22-06/21)	♊	Cancer (06/22-07/22)	♋
Leo (07/23-08/22)	♌	Virgo (08/23-09/23)	♍	Libra (09/24-10/23)	♎	Scorpio (10/24-11/22)	♏
Sagittarius (11/23-12/21)	♐	Capricorn (12/22-01/20)	♑	Aquarius (01/21-02/18)	♒	Pisces (02/19-03/20)	♓

Where do you live?

Are you in any school clubs?

C *Listen to the short conversations. Which club does the person join? Check the correct pictures.*
CD 1-10

①

②

What's Your Zodiac Sign?

A *Watch the video clip and check the correct answers.* WEB動画

1. What's James's major?
- ☐ **a.** Law
- ☐ **b.** Physics
- ☐ **c.** Marketing

2. Why does Cherry need James's help?
- ☐ **a.** She's very interested in marketing.
- ☐ **b.** Her major is not actually physics.
- ☐ **c.** She's having difficulty with the project.

3. Where will Cherry and James meet?
- ☐ **a.** Cherry's dorm
- ☐ **b.** The school library
- ☐ **c.** The school cafeteria

4. What does James want to do after they study?
- ☐ **a.** Go to the library and have coffee with Cherry
- ☐ **b.** Get a drink and watch TV with Cherry
- ☐ **c.** Go to dinner and see a film with Cherry

My major is marketing. You?

I'm a physics major.

B *Listen to the conversation and fill in the blanks.* 🎧 1-11 📺

James: Hello, I'm James. The teacher told me I'm one of your [1]_____ for the research project. Nice to meet you.

Cherry: Hi, I'm Cherry. It's a pleasure to meet you. Welcome to the group.

James: Thanks. What's your major?

Cherry: My major is marketing. You?

James: I'm a [2]_____ major. Just out of curiosity, what's your zodiac sign?

Cherry: I'm a Leo. My younger brother says that's why I'm so [3]_____.

James: They do say that about Leos.

Cherry: I think star signs are interesting. But I need to [4]_____ on this project because I'm really struggling.

James: Well, maybe I can help you after class.

Cherry: Wow, thanks! I really appreciate it, James. Where do you want to meet?

James: We can meet at the school [5]_____ if that's convenient for you. Where do you live?

Cherry: I live in the [6]_____, so that works for me. It's only about a 15-minute walk.

James: Great. If you have time after we're done studying, why don't we get a [7]_____ to eat and see a movie?

Cherry: Whoa! Slow down. I'm just looking for a partner, not a [8]_____.

C *Practice the conversation with your partner.*

D *Listen to the conversation and check the correct answers.* 🎧 1-12

		Emily		Simon
Major	☐	English	☐	English
	☐	marketing	☐	marketing
School Club	☐	English	☐	English
	☐	dance	☐	dance

Be Verbs (Wh- + am/are/is + S. ?)

Why are you in the dance club?

Because I like dancing.

Question	Response
Where are you?	I'm <u>at the library</u>.
Where is Ben from?	He's <u>from England</u>.
When is your birthday?	My birthday is <u>on May 12</u>.

Base Verbs (Wh- + do/does + S. + V. ?)

Why does Mark study so much?

Because he has a test tomorrow.

Question	Response
Where do you live?	I live <u>in an apartment near my school</u>.
Where does Mike study?	He studies <u>at ABC University</u>.
When do we have English class?	We have English class <u>on Mondays</u>.
When does the test start?	It starts <u>in 10 minutes</u>.
Why do you know her?	Because <u>she's my classmate</u>.

Work It Out

Ⓐ *Match the questions with the answers.*

① Who's that chubby boy?   •   • Because I have to study for an exam.

② What's your name?   •   • He works at a school.

③ Where does your father work?   •   • He's my brother Nick.

④ Why do you stay at home all day? •   • He comes home at six o'clock.

⑤ When does your father come home? •   • My name is Sandy.

Ⓑ *Read the answers. Write the questions based on the <u>underlined words</u>.*

① *What is your major?*
My major is <u>English</u>.

② _____
She lives <u>in the dorm</u>.

③ _____
I'm in the English club <u>because I like to study English</u>.

an action which is happening at the time of speaking

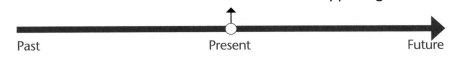

Past   Present   Future

Affirmatives | S. + am/are/is + V-ing | **Negatives** | S. + am/are/is + not + V-ing

Yes, I am.

Are you studying?

No, I'm not. I'm **listening** to music.

Yes/No Questions

Question	"Yes" Response	"No" Response
Is he **playing** baseball?	Yes, he is.	No, he's not. He's **playing** basketball.
Are they **singing** karaoke?	Yes, they are.	No, they aren't. They're **studying**.

Wh- Questions

Question	Response
What **is** she **doing** now?	She's **doing** the laundry.
Who **is making** popcorn?	My sister **is** (**making** popcorn).

Spelling changes with V-ing	
Add -ing	sing → singing
Double the consonant and add -ing	sit → sitting
Drop –e and add -ing	come → coming

Work It Out

A *Complete the dialogue based on the hints given.*

A: What is Grace ___doing___ (do) now?

B: She's _____ (wash) the dishes.

A: Billy is _____ (swim). Alice is _____ (paint) pictures for her homework. Are you _____ (come) with me?

B: Sure.

B *Answer the questions based on the pictures.*

1.

Is he driving?
_____
Does he drive?
_____
What does he do?
_____

2.

Is she cooking?
_____
Does she cook?
_____
What does she do?
_____

3.

Are they teaching?
_____
Do they teach?
_____
What do they do?
_____

FLIPPED CLASSROOM

🎧 1-13

You already know the traditional teaching method. During class time, teachers do all the talking. Students listen, take notes, and ask questions. At home, students do their homework. Now, some teachers are using a very different style. Before class, students listen to their teacher's lecture at home. Usually, they watch a video 5 on their computers. When students are in class, they do homework activities. The teacher guides the students. The name of this new teaching method is the "flipped classroom." The flipped classroom teaching style is becoming very popular.

Here's the main idea of the flipped classroom method: when you want to teach someone, you shouldn't just fill their heads with information. You should 10 also teach them to use that information. When you use new knowledge, it's easier to remember. Also, you can understand why that knowledge is important. Finally, you learn to think in new ways. One U.S. high school flipped all its classes. The results were interesting. Many students who had problems before became the best students in class.

TRADITIONAL	FLIPPED
Lecture / Homework activities	Lecture / Classroom activites

A *Fill in the blanks with the word choices given. Change the word form if necessary.*

| method / lecture / traditional / flip / knowledge |

1. Charles has a wide _____ of music.
2. Jill _____ the book open and started to read.
3. It's _____ in America to eat turkey on Thanksgiving Day.
4. What _____ of payment do you prefer? Cash or credit card?
5. We went to a _____ on American history.

B *Check the correct answers.*

1. In the traditional teaching method, what do students do?
   ☐ **a.** Listen, take notes, and ask questions
   ☐ **b.** Talk all the time
   ☐ **c.** Do homework during class time

2. In the new style, when do students listen to lectures?
   ☐ **a.** When they are in class
   ☐ **b.** When they are at home
   ☐ **c.** When they are in the library

3. What's happening to the flipped classroom method?
   ☐ **a.** More and more people are using it.
   ☐ **b.** Fewer and fewer people are using it.
   ☐ **c.** People are changing it all the time.

4. When teachers use the flipped classroom method, what do they do?
   ☐ **a.** They teach students how to use information.
   ☐ **b.** They just fill students' heads with information.
   ☐ **c.** They learn things from the students.

5. What happens when you use knowledge?
   ☐ **a.** You forget it more quickly.
   ☐ **b.** You learn it more slowly.
   ☐ **c.** You learn it more easily.

A *Read the ad and answer the questions.*

ENGLISH CLUB

SPEAKING ENGLISH IS FUN!

Do you enjoy learning and using English?
Do you need help with your English homework? Then, the English Club is for you!

- -

Come improve your English HERE!

☆ In the English Club, we meet native English speakers and use English to play games and make friends.

☆ The English Club is open to all students.

☆ We meet every Tuesday and Thursday, from 4:30 to 6:00, in Classroom E7.

For more information, please e-mail us at EnglishClub@buxton.edu.hn.

① What do students do in the English Club?

_____

② Who can join the English Club?

_____

③ When do students go to the English Club?

_____

④ Where do students go if they want to join the English Club?

_____

B *Write questions about Ken and Joan for the following answers. Focus on the underlined words.*

① Where are Ken and Joan from?

They are from Canada.

② _____

They are studying.

③ _____

They live in the dorm.

④ _____

They have marketing class on Fridays.

28

CHALLENGE YOURSELF

Part I Pictures 🎧 1-14

Look at the picture and choose the best answer.

1.

☐ a   ☐ b   ☐ c

2.

☐ a   ☐ b   ☐ c

Part II Question & Response 🎧 1-15

Listen to the statement or question and choose the best response.

3. ☐ a   ☐ b   ☐ c   5. ☐ a   ☐ b   ☐ c
4. ☐ a   ☐ b   ☐ c   6. ☐ a   ☐ b   ☐ c

Part III Conversations 🎧 1-16

Listen to the conversation and answer the questions.

7. What are they talking about?
   ☐ a. What they study in school
   ☐ b. Their favorite hobby
   ☐ c. What they want to learn

8. What did the woman say?
   ☐ a. She lives in the dorm.
   ☐ b. She lives next to the
       supermarket.
   ☐ c. She often goes to the
       supermarket.

9. What does the woman want to
   know?
   ☐ a. How much money the man
       makes
   ☐ b. Whether the man is married
   ☐ c. How old the man is and the
       zodiac he belongs to

10. What does the man mean?
   ☐ a. He needs to start the report.
   ☐ b. He has to get help on the
       report.
   ☐ c. He has to complete the report.

Linguaporta Training

Let's review the unit with Linguaporta.

WARM UP

PICTURE DICTIONARY

Listen to the sentences and match the pictures to the correct numbers. 🔊 1-17

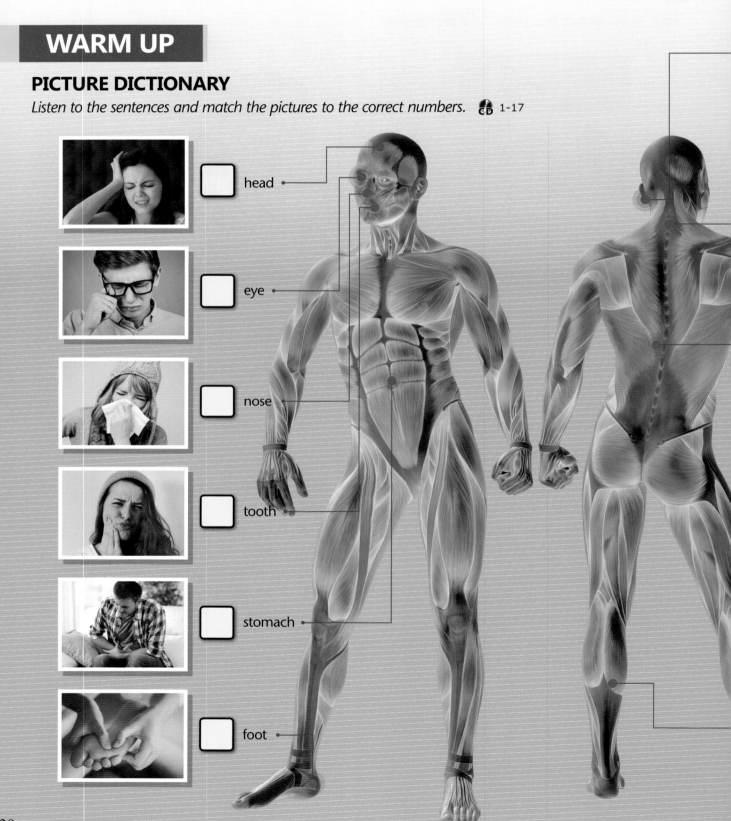

head

eye

nose

tooth

stomach

foot

ear

neck

back

arm

hand

leg

SET IN MOTION

A *Role-play with a partner. Use the vocabulary you have learned.*

Ⓐ What's wrong?

Ⓑ My _____ hurts.

= I have a sore _____.

Ⓐ You should go to see a doctor.

B *Listen to the sentences. Match the people with their health problems.* 🎧 1-18

a toothache	a sore arm
a headache	sore legs
a backache	a stomachache

① James has _____.

② Amy has _____.

③ Ben has _____.

④ Megan has _____.

⑤ Sam has _____.

⑥ Jeff has _____.

31

What's the Matter?

A *Watch the video clip and check the correct answers.* WEB動画 🖥️

1. Where was Marty?
   - ☐ **a.** At the hospital
   - ☐ **b.** At the doctor's house
   - ☐ **c.** At his house

2. What's the matter with Marty?
   - ☐ **a.** His leg hurts.
   - ☐ **b.** He's sick.
   - ☐ **c.** He has a toothache.

3. What happened when Tim visited Marty?
   - ☐ **a.** Marty felt better.
   - ☐ **b.** Tim felt sick.
   - ☐ **c.** Marty called the doctor.

4. What did the doctor do for Tim?
   - ☐ **a.** He gave Tim some advice.
   - ☐ **b.** He gave Tim some medicine.
   - ☐ **c.** He said Tim should rest.

B *Listen to the conversation and fill in the blanks.* 🎧 1-19 📺

Amber is at home when Tim comes back.

Amber: Hi, Tim. Where were you?

Tim: I was at the hospital. I went to see a doctor.

Amber: You did? Why? What's the matter?

Tim: Well, I visited my friend Marty at his [1]_____. He's really sick.

Amber: What's [2]_____ with him?

Tim: He has a stomachache, a sore [3]_____, a fever, and a headache.

Amber: That's terrible! But then why did you go to see a doctor?

Tim: Marty told me about his stomachache. Then my stomach [4]_____.

Amber: That's strange.

Tim: Yeah. Then Marty told me about his headache and his sore throat.

Amber: Let me [5]_____. Your head hurt and your throat became sore.

Tim: That's right. Then I got a [6]_____! I felt so sick! So I went to see the doctor.

Amber: What did the doctor say? Are you really sick?

Tim: No, I'm not sick at all. The doctor made me feel better.

Amber: What did he do? Did he give you some [7]_____?

Tim: No, he gave me some [8]_____. He told me to stop visiting sick people!

C *Practice the conversation with your partner.*

D *Listen to the conversation. Number the health problems they are talking about from 1 to 4.* 🎧 1-20

☐ headache   ☐ fever

☐ cough   ☐ dizzy

GRAMMAR **1 Past Simple — Be Verbs**

Affirmatives `S. + was/were` **Negatives** `S. + was/were + not`

Past — He **was** heavy. Now — He is skinny.

Past — My parents **were** young. Now — My parents are old.

am / is → was

are → were

Yes/No Questions

Question	"Yes" Response	"No" Response
Were you a nurse?	Yes, I was. I worked at a hospital.	No, I wasn't. I was a doctor.
Was she skinny?	Yes, she was. She exercised every day.	No, she wasn't. She was chubby.

Wh- Questions

Question	Response
Where were you?	I was in the library.
How was your weekend?	It was fun. I went to the movies with Nancy.

Work It Out

A *Answer the questions based on the hints given.*

① Were you short during junior high school?
   Yes, I was. / No, I wasn't. I was tall.

② Was he a taxi driver? (No / teacher)
   _____

③ Were Dad and Mom at home? (Yes)
   _____

④ Were they in the library? (No / at the coffee shop)
   _____

was not = wasn't
were not = weren't

B *Fill in the blanks with **was** or **were** and complete the sentences.*

① A: _____ you at home yesterday?
   B: Yes, I _____.

② She _____ skinny before, but she is chubby now.

③ They _____ worried about their daughter.

④ _____ you happy at the party?

34

GRAMMAR **2 Past Simple — Base Verbs**

an action that happened in the past

Past — Present — Future

2020

NOW 2021

She lived in France last year.

Yes/No Questions

Question	"Yes" Response	"No" Response
Did you **live** in France?	Yes, I **did**.	No, I **didn't**.
Did she **go** to London by subway?	Yes, she **did**.	No, she **didn't**.
Did they **grow up** in Japan?	Yes, they **did**.	No, they **didn't**.

Wh- Questions

Question	Response
Where **did** they come from?	They **came** from the store.
How **did** you go to school?	I **went** to school by bus.

Work It Out

Ⓐ *Complete the paragraph based on the hints given. Change the verb form if necessary.*

It ¹_____ (be) cool and windy last weekend. On Saturday morning, my family ²_____ (go) to the beach. We ³_____ (go) cycling and swimming. After that, we ⁴_____ (have) a barbecue at the beach. When we ⁵_____ (come) home, we ⁶_____ (be) tired, but we still ⁷_____ (play) cards until midnight. On Sunday morning, we ⁸_____ (get) up early and ⁹_____ (go) rock climbing. In the mountains, we ¹⁰_____ (take) lots of beautiful photos. On Sunday evening, we ¹¹_____ (see) a movie and ¹²_____ (eat) dinner at a nice restaurant. The weekend was fun, and we really ¹³_____ (enjoy) it.

Ⓑ *Answer the questions in complete sentences based on the hints given.*

① Did you play soccer yesterday afternoon? (No / play baseball)

No, I didn't. I played baseball.

② Did Megan wear a skirt yesterday? (Yes)

_____

③ Did Jerry read a book last night? (No / surf the Internet)

_____

Regular Verbs		Irregular Verbs
• -ed / -d	walk → walked	do → did
	change → changed	eat → ate
		get → got
		go → went
• -ied	study → studied	take → took
		wear → wore

35

🎧 1-21

Patient Information Form

First Name		Middle Name		Last Name	
Ryan		Vincent		Mason	

Age	Date of Birth	Sex	Marital Status
19	01/15/2002	☑ Male ☐ Female	☑ Single ☐ Married

Home Phone	Cell Phone	E-mail Address
123-456-789	987-654-321	ryan_mason@abc.com

Address
432 Middlebury St., Boston, MA 02131

Emergency Contact	Emergency Contact Number	Emergency Contact Relationship
Elaine Mason	012-234-567	mother

Health History	Allergy
Heart problems	Penicillin

What are your symptoms?

My stomach is really bothering me. I cough and sneeze a lot. I feel very tired.

Please fill out this form and turn it in at the registration desk. Be sure to inform the nurse of all allergies.

Doctor's advice:

Take medicine three times a day, after meals. Drink plenty of water and avoid heavy foods.

A *Fill in the blanks with the word choices given. Change the word form if necessary.*

> fill out / bother / emergency / patient / inform

1. This door should only be used in a(n) _____.
2. Jim went to _____ his boss of his decision.
3. The _____ has a severe heart condition.
4. It _____ me when people smoke in restaurants.
5. To get a passport, you have to _____ all these papers.

B *Check the correct answers.*

1. What is wrong with Ryan?
   - ☐ a. He has a headache.
   - ☐ b. He has a sore throat.
   - ☐ c. He has a stomachache.

2. Who is Elaine?
   - ☐ a. Ryan's wife
   - ☐ b. Ryan's mother
   - ☐ c. Ryan's doctor

3. What is the doctor's advice to Ryan?
   - ☐ a. Inform the nurse of his allergy.
   - ☐ b. Eat some heavy foods.
   - ☐ c. Drink a lot of water.

4. Can Ryan be given penicillin?
   - ☐ a. Yes, he can. No problem.
   - ☐ b. No, he can't. He's allergic to it.
   - ☐ c. No information.

5. Which is true about the form?
   - ☐ a. Ryan Mason was born in January.
   - ☐ b. Ryan Mason has had a history of stomach problems.
   - ☐ c. Ryan Mason should take medicine twice a day.

WRITING

A *Rewrite the following sentences as negative sentences and questions.*

① Mary got up at seven o'clock.

  Mary didn't get up at seven o'clock.   _Did Mary get up at seven o'clock?_

② Henry did his homework.

  _____   _____

③ Tim was in the cafeteria.

  _____   _____

④ Sarah had a stomachache.

  _____   _____

⑤ They studied in the library.

  _____   _____

B *Read the patient information form and answer the questions.*

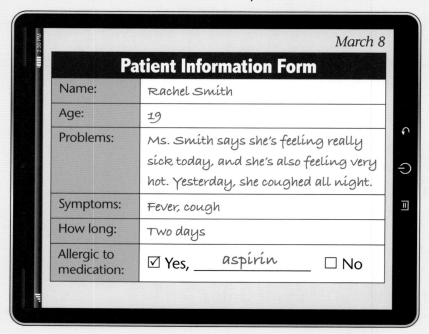

March 8

Patient Information Form

Name:	Rachel Smith
Age:	19
Problems:	Ms. Smith says she's feeling really sick today, and she's also feeling very hot. Yesterday, she coughed all night.
Symptoms:	Fever, cough
How long:	Two days
Allergic to medication:	☑ Yes, _aspirin_ ☐ No

① How is Rachel feeling today?

  _____

② What are Rachel's symptoms?

  _____

③ When did her problems start?

  _____

④ Is Rachel allergic to any forms of medication?

  _____

CHALLENGE YOURSELF

Part I Pictures   1-22

Look at the picture and choose the best answer.

1.

☐ a   ☐ b   ☐ c

2.

☐ a   ☐ b   ☐ c

Part II Question & Response   1-23

Listen to the statement or question and choose the best response.

3. ☐ a   ☐ b   ☐ c   5. ☐ a   ☐ b   ☐ c
4. ☐ a   ☐ b   ☐ c   6. ☐ a   ☐ b   ☐ c

Part III Conversations   1-24

Listen to the conversation and answer the questions.

7. What did Ryan do last night?
    ☐ a. He went out with his girlfriend.
    ☐ b. He went to the movies.
    ☐ c. He watched a video.

8. How long was the cat gone?
    ☐ a. Since Vincent went to work today.
    ☐ b. For a few days.
    ☐ c. Since this morning.

9. What is the woman saying?
    ☐ a. Her throat hurts.
    ☐ b. She's feeling OK.
    ☐ c. She has medicine.

10. What does the woman say about Ron?
    ☐ a. He's sleeping.
    ☐ b. He's sick.
    ☐ c. He's working.

Linguaporta Training

Let's review the unit with Linguaporta.

WARM UP

PICTURE DICTIONARY

Listen to the sentences and match the pictures to the correct numbers. 🎧 1-25

afraid

angry

shy

sad

nervous

pleased

surprised

bored

excited

lonely

proud

happy

SET IN MOTION

Ⓐ *Role-play with a partner. Use the vocabulary you have learned.*

A: Where were you last night?

B: I was at a pop concert.

A: Were you _____?

B: No, I wasn't _____. I was _____.

Ⓑ *Listen to the sentences again and fill in the blanks with words you have learned.*

1. I'm too _____ to meet new people.

2. Sarah was _____ to see the concert.

3. Albert was very _____ of his daughter when she won an English contest.

4. Karen is _____, so she wants to make new friends.

5. Nancy felt very _____ at the news.

6. Holly was very _____ about the test.

7. George is _____ because his father is sick.

8. Peter is _____ to help you out.

9. Susan is _____ of spiders.

10. When I'm _____, I listen to the radio.

11. Henry is _____ with me for breaking his laptop.

12. I'm very _____ with my new house.

41

CONVERSATION

How Was Last Weekend?

A *Watch the video clip and check the correct answers.* WEB動画 📺💻

1. Did Betty enjoy her weekend?
   - ☐ **a.** Yes, she felt it was exciting.
   - ☐ **b.** No, she felt it wasn't boring.
   - ☐ **c.** No, she felt it wasn't exciting.

2. Who did Betty go to the amusement park with?
   - ☐ **a.** Kenny
   - ☐ **b.** Lenny
   - ☐ **c.** Dave

3. How did Betty think the rides were?
   - ☐ **a.** She thought they were boring.
   - ☐ **b.** She thought they were funny.
   - ☐ **c.** She thought they were small.

4. What did Betty think about Dave before?
   - ☐ **a.** He was very shy.
   - ☐ **b.** He was very jealous.
   - ☐ **c.** He was very boring.

What's up? How was last weekend?

It wasn't that exciting.

42

B *Listen to the conversation and fill in the blanks.* 🎧 1-26 💻

Dave: What's up? How was last weekend? Where were you?

Betty: It wasn't that ¹_____. I just went to an amusement park on Saturday.

Dave: Oh, yeah? That sounds exciting.

Betty: Well, I wanted to go on some cool rides, but it wasn't to be.

Dave: Why? What happened?

Betty: The amusement park only had rides for small children. It was pretty
²_____.

Dave: Was Kenny with you at the amusement park?

Betty: No, not Kenny. I went with his brother Lenny.

Dave: What? Did you ³_____ up with Kenny?

Betty: No, not yet. I was ⁴_____ with Kenny, so I went with his brother Lenny instead. I just wanted to make Kenny jealous.

Dave: Really? Did it work?

Betty: Not at all. He wasn't even a bit ⁵_____. He knows I think Lenny is boring.

Dave: Yeah, Lenny is not the best ⁶_____. I know how you can teach Kenny a lesson. Go out with me this Saturday. We'll have a great time!

Betty: I'm surprised at you, Dave. I always thought you were ⁷_____.

Dave: I guess you didn't understand the ⁸_____ me.

Betty: OK then, let's do it. Just tell me the time and place, and I'll be there.

C *Practice the conversation with your partner.*

D *Listen to the two short conversations and the questions. Check the correct pictures.* 🎧 1-27

① ☐ bored ☐ excited ② ☐ shy ☐ proud

43

Present Simple VS. Past Simple

Habit		Past action
	VS.	
They go jogging every morning.		They went jogging in the afternoon yesterday.

True		True in the past
	VS.	
Mandy likes vegetables.		Mandy didn't like vegetables when she was a kid.

Present Simple VS. Present Continuous

Habit		Action that is happening
	VS.	
Cecilia often plays tennis on the weekend.		Cecilia is playing tennis.

Permanent situation		Temporary situation
	VS.	
The family lives in Tokyo.		Alice is studying abroad.

Verbs that cannot be used in the present continuous tense

Related to "desire"	dislike, hate, like, love
Related to "thinking"	believe, know, mean, understand
Related to "sense"	feel, hear, see, smell, taste
Related to "possession"	belong, have, own, possess

ex.)
- I **love** the smell of fresh mangoes.
- Joseph **believes** that ghosts exist.

UNIT 04

EXPRESSING YOURSELF

Work It Out

A *Fill in the blanks based on the hints given.*

① My father _____ (live) in the countryside when he _____ (be) little. After I was born, our family _____ (move) to the big city.

② I _____ (not like) to eat bread in the morning, so my mother _____ (make) some noodle soup for me right now.

③ The students _____ (do) their homework right now. They _____ (have) a lot to do.

B *Use the correct form of the words to fill in the blanks.*

Vincent was fat and liked to eat sweets. He usually _____ (eat) more than five meals a day and always _____ (order) greasy meals from restaurants. After he failed to find a girlfriend for many years, he _____ (decide) to lose weight. He now _____ (jog) every day, _____ (eat) only vegetables and lean meat, and _____ (go) to the gym whenever he has time. He _____ (have) a girlfriend now. She goes to the gym with him.

C *Write O if the sentence is correct. If not, write X.*

_____ ① Are you knowing that pretty girl over there?

_____ ② Jennifer said she really likes your new haircut.

_____ ③ They are owning their own house.

_____ ④ I think I understand how to solve this problem.

What "Color" Are You?

 1-28

Before you can express yourself well, you need to know yourself. What situations make you nervous or shy? Are you bored with day-to-day life, or do you wake up excited each morning?

Many people learn about what makes them happy or sad by taking
5   online personality tests. One well-known test is the Color Code Personality Test.

During the test, the user answers questions such as, "Do you think people are jealous of you because you are happy?" or, "Are you afraid of not having a career plan?" Afterwards, the computer program groups the
10 user into one of four colors—red, blue, white, and yellow. People who are "reds" want power, "blues" want romance, "white" want peace, and "yellow" want fun.

People might not be proud of the results—they might even make the users a little angry. But most people who take the test are pleased to get
15 an honest opinion about themselves. Are you interested in this test? Surf the Internet now!

A *Fill in the blanks with the word choices given. Change the word form if necessary.*

> express / jealous / pleased / career / situation

1. When I grow up, I'll have a _____ as a teacher.
2. Billy is in a difficult _____ at the moment.
3. Words cannot _____ how happy I am.
4. My teacher wasn't _____ with my math score.
5. You're just _____ of Peter's success.

B *Check the correct answers.*

1. Based on the article, how do many people learn about themselves?
   ☐ **a.** By making themselves happy every day
   ☐ **b.** By answering questions from friends
   ☐ **c.** By taking personality tests online

2. What kind of personality test does the article talk about?
   ☐ **a.** A Color Code Personality Test
   ☐ **b.** A Color Change Personality Test
   ☐ **c.** A User Code Personality Test

3. Which color is NOT included in the personality test?
   ☐ **a.** White
   ☐ **b.** Blue
   ☐ **c.** Green

4. What do people who are "yellow" want?
   ☐ **a.** Peace
   ☐ **b.** Fun
   ☐ **c.** Power

5. After people find out the results, how do they feel about them?
   ☐ **a.** They are very proud of the results they get.
   ☐ **b.** They are not angry about the results at all.
   ☐ **c.** They are pleased to get an honest opinion.

WRITING

A *Read Lily's diary and fill in the blanks with the words below.*

better / shy / angry / tired / afraid

DATE: May 25

Dear Diary,

   Today, I really had bad luck. I woke up late and missed the bus. My teacher got ¹_____ when I walked into class 30 minutes late. I sat down in my seat and felt nervous. During lunchtime, I discovered I had left my lunch money at home. Watching my classmates eat, I felt sad, but I was too ²_____ to borrow money. On my way home, a big dog started to chase me. Feeling ³_____, I ran away as fast as I could, so I was really ⁴_____ when I got home. Unfortunately, I tripped and fell, ripping my pants. I hope tomorrow is ⁵_____.

Love,

Me

B *Write a short diary about yourself. Use Lily's diary as an example.*

DATE: _____

Dear Diary,

_____

_____

_____

_____

_____

_____

Love,

Me

CHALLENGE YOURSELF

Part I Pictures 🔊 1-29

Look at the picture and choose the best answer.

1.

☐ a   ☐ b   ☐ c

2.

☐ a   ☐ b   ☐ c

Part II Question & Response 🔊 1-30

Listen to the statement or question and choose the best response.

3. ☐ a   ☐ b   ☐ c   5. ☐ a   ☐ b   ☐ c
4. ☐ a   ☐ b   ☐ c   6. ☐ a   ☐ b   ☐ c

Part III Conversations 🔊 1-31

Listen to the conversation and answer the questions.

7. How does she feel?
   ☐ a. Lonely
   ☐ b. Pleased
   ☐ c. Tired

8. How did the woman feel when she met Tom Cruise?
   ☐ a. She felt sad.
   ☐ b. She felt bored.
   ☐ c. She felt nervous.

9. How does Brent describe himself?
   ☐ a. He says he's expressive.
   ☐ b. He says he's stupid.
   ☐ c. He says he's shy.

10. What does the man tell the woman to do?
    ☐ a. Tell him what happened
    ☐ b. Call the police
    ☐ c. Try not to be mad

Linguaporta Training

Let's review the unit with Linguaporta.

49

UNIT 05

Getting Around

WARM UP

PICTURE DICTIONARY

Listen to the sentences. Write the sentence number in the correct boxes below. 🎧 1-32

☐ scooter

☐ helicopter

☐ bus

☐ train

☐ bicycle

SET IN MOTION

Ⓐ *Role-play with a partner. Use the vocabulary you have learned.*

Ⓐ How do you get to school every day?

Ⓑ I get to school by _____.

Ⓐ How long does it take you to get to school?

Ⓑ It takes about _____ minutes.

Ⓑ *Listen to the sentences again and fill in the blanks with words you have learned.*

1. That _____ was very loud when it landed.

2. Dave is excited about driving his new _____.

3. An _____ carried the injured man to the hospital.

V.	+	Transportation
ride	a	bicycle / scooter / motorcycle
drive	a	car
take	a(n)	airplane / helicopter / bus / taxi / train

airplane

car

taxi

motorcycle

ambulance

ship

4. Henry isn't afraid to ride his _____ in the rain.

5. It's very expensive to take an _____ these days.

6. Heather enjoys riding her new _____.

7. What time does the next _____ leave for London?

8. The _____ sailed to South America.

9. Pamela takes the _____ to work every day.

10. Riding a _____ is fun and good exercise, too.

11. The cost of taking a _____ will go up with the increase in the price of gas.

The World Traveler

Ⓐ *Watch the video clip and check the correct answers.* 📺

1. What is one way the woman doesn't travel?
   - ☐ **a.** By plane
   - ☐ **b.** By train
   - ☐ **c.** By bus

2. Which is the woman's favorite way to travel?
   - ☐ **a.** By train
   - ☐ **b.** By bicycle
   - ☐ **c.** On foot

3. How did the woman travel in Africa?
   - ☐ **a.** By bicycle
   - ☐ **b.** By car
   - ☐ **c.** By plane

4. Which trip was the most exciting for the woman?
   - ☐ **a.** Her trip to Mexico
   - ☐ **b.** Her trip to India
   - ☐ **c.** Her trip to Africa

Welcome to the show.

Thank you.

B *Listen to the conversation and fill in the blanks.* **CD** 1-33 💻

A TV host is interviewing Maggie Jenkins.

Host: Today, we are talking to world traveler Maggie Jenkins. Welcome to the show, Maggie.

Maggie: Thank you. It's a ¹_____ to be here.

Host: When you travel, I think you use many different ²_____ of transportation.

Maggie: That's right. On my trips, I travel by boat, by train, by bus, and even by bicycle.

Host: What is your favorite form of transportation?

Maggie: Well, my favorite form is right here: my own two ³_____. Last year, I went from Alaska to Mexico on foot.

Host: That's ⁴_____! I don't even walk to work, and you walk across countries!

The TV host asks Maggie some questions about her trips.

Host: Which trip was the most exciting, Maggie?

Maggie: My trip to Africa was the most exciting. I traveled by ⁵_____ most of the time.

Host: Most of the time? What other forms of transportation did you use?

Maggie: Well, I took ⁶_____ buses and trains.

Host: What is the most interesting form of transportation you used?

Maggie: In India, I rode a camel in the ⁷_____.

Host: But a camel isn't a form of transportation.

Maggie: Sure it is. Many people still use animals to get around. They ⁸_____ animals to the market and even to school!

Host: Cool!

C *Practice the conversation with your partner.*

D *Listen to the three short conversations and number the vehicles the speakers take 1 to 3.* **CD** 1-34

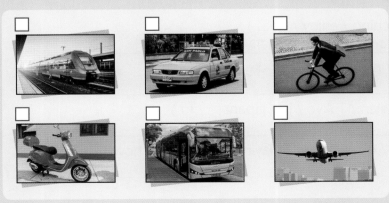

Infinitives (to V.)

- **To learn math well** is hard.
  = It's hard **to learn math well**.
    ↳ *as a subject*

- Timmy likes **to camp** in the summer.
    ↳ *as an object of a verb*

- My mom wants me **to do** the laundry.
    ↳ *as a complement*

* **not + to V.**
   My doctor warned me not to eat too much.

Gerunds (V-ing)

- **Riding a bike** is interesting.
    ↳ *as a subject*

- Can you finish **cleaning the bathroom**
  by five o'clock?
    ↳ *as an object of a verb*

- Neil's favorite sport is **swimming**.
    ↳ *as a complement*

* **go + V-ing**
   We go camping every summer.

★Verbs followed by an infinitive		
agree	ask	continue
decide	expect	hope
plan	promise	want

- Audrey wants to go on a vacation.
- My mother needs to buy some groceries.

★Verbs followed by a gerund		
avoid	can't help	deny
enjoy	mind	practice
quit		

- I enjoy watching TV after school.

★Verbs followed by an infinitive or a gerund		
begin	hate	like
love	start	

- I love reading. = I love to read.

Work It Out

A *Fill in the blanks with the correct form of the verb.*

① Luke enjoys _____ to music. (listen)

② The students hope _____ the exam. (pass)

③ I plan _____ abroad. (work)

④ Do you mind _____ the window? (open)

⑤ I can't help _____ when Kate makes funny faces at me. (laugh)

B *Rearrange the sentences.*

① (TV / Nicole / watching / enjoy / does)
   Does Nicole enjoy watching TV _____ ?

② (to / Jody / every / plans / exercise / day)
   _____ .

③ (wants / study / Helen / Tokyo / in / Japanese / to)
   _____ .

④ (Darren / practice / does / often / playing / the piano / how)
   _____ ?

In/On/By

> S. + { go / get } + to + places + { by + all means of transportation / in + a car/van/truck/taxi / on + a train/plane/bus/ship/bike/motorcycle/foot }

How do you go to school?

I go to school by bike.
How about you?

By skateboard.

- Nancy goes to the library **by** bike.
- I go to school **on** foot.

To

> S. + { take + all means of transportation / ride + a horse/bicycle/motorcycle / drive + a car/van/truck } + to + places

A: How do you go to school?

B: I ride a bike to school.   = I go to school by bike.   = By bike.

Work It Out

A *Fill in the blanks with **on** or **in**.*

① I usually go to school _____ my scooter.

② Tim always goes to work _____ a taxi.

③ Jane got _____ the bus and paid her fare.

④ Grandpa took me for a ride _____ his big truck.

B *Look at the pictures and answer the questions.*

① How does Emma go to the park?

② How does Mr. Lee go to work?

③ How does Jason go to church?

_____   _____   _____

55

🎧 1-35

How We Should Use Priority Seats

You're sitting on the bus. An elderly person boards the bus. All the seats are full, so the elderly person must stand. In that situation, you should give your seat to the elderly person. However, some people aren't willing to give up their seats. Some people pretend they don't notice the elderly person. Some people
5 even pretend to be asleep! This behavior is not proper. These days, most buses and subways have priority seats. Priority seats are special seats for people in need.

If you see a young man in a priority seat on the train, don't assume he's selfish. He perhaps has a health problem you can't see. What if you're in a
10 regular seat? Should you still give your seat to someone in need? Of course you should! Put yourself in the other person's shoes. When you are tired or in pain, you don't want to stand, do you? You shouldn't give up your seat just because you have to obey the rules. You should do it because generosity and kindness can help people.

Priority Seating

Ⓐ *Fill in the blanks with the word choices given. Change the word form if necessary.*

> obey / generosity / be willing to / board / pretend

1. We _____ the airplane at seven o'clock yesterday.

2. You have to _____ the rules.

3. The king was famous for his _____.

4. Let's _____ we've never met before.

5. Amy _____ teach me French, but I want to learn English.

Ⓑ *Check the correct answers.*

1. Based on the article, why would an elderly person stand?
   - ☐ **a.** The subway didn't stop at the station.
   - ☐ **b.** There are no more seats in the bus.
   - ☐ **c.** They don't want to sit.

2. Why won't some people give up their seats?
   - ☐ **a.** They didn't notice they sat in a priority seat.
   - ☐ **b.** They can't see any elderly people.
   - ☐ **c.** They don't want to give up their seat.

3. Why might it be OK for young people to sit in a priority seat?
   - ☐ **a.** They might have a health problem.
   - ☐ **b.** They might not have any elderly family members.
   - ☐ **c.** They might not be very generous.

4. What does "Put yourself in the other person's shoes" mean?
   - ☐ **a.** Wear the other person's shoes.
   - ☐ **b.** Give your shoes to another person.
   - ☐ **c.** Imagine you're in the other person's situation.

5. Why should you give up your seat, even if it's a regular seat?
   - ☐ **a.** Because somebody will think you are selfish.
   - ☐ **b.** Because you want to help people in need.
   - ☐ **c.** Because you want to obey the rules only.

WRITING

A *Look at the boarding pass and answer the questions below.*

① What is the passenger's full name?

② What flight is the passenger taking?

③ What gate does the passenger need to go to?

④ What time does the flight board?

⑤ Where is the passenger traveling to?

B *Tell your classmates what you like to do and what you enjoy doing. Write four sentences.*

① I'm not good at sports, but I like to watch them.

②

③

④

⑤

CHALLENGE YOURSELF

Part I Pictures 🎧 1-36

Look at the picture and choose the best answer.

1.

☐ a ☐ b ☐ c

2.

☐ a ☐ b ☐ c

Part II Question & Response 🎧 1-37

Listen to the statement or question and choose the best response.

3. ☐ a ☐ b ☐ c   5. ☐ a ☐ b ☐ c
4. ☐ a ☐ b ☐ c   6. ☐ a ☐ b ☐ c

Part III Conversations 🎧 1-38

Listen to the conversation and answer the questions.

7. What are the man and woman
   looking at?
   ☐ a. Something in the air
   ☐ b. Something in the water
   ☐ c. Something on the road

8. What will they probably do next?
   ☐ a. Go to a party
   ☐ b. Buy a new coat
   ☐ c. Go to the supermarket

9. How did the woman travel?
   ☐ a. She drove.
   ☐ b. She took the train.
   ☐ c. She went by plane.

10. What does the woman have to do?
    ☐ a. She has to take a test.
    ☐ b. She has to go shopping.
    ☐ c. She has to catch a plane.

Linguaporta Training

Let's review the unit with Linguaporta.

Talking about the Time

WARM UP

PICTURE DICTIONARY

Listen to the sentences. Each sentence is about a month of the year. Write the sentence number in the correct boxes below. 🔊 1-39

❄ JANUARY

Sun	Mon	Tue	Wed	Thu	Fri	Sat
	1	2	3	4	5	6
7	8	9	10	11	12	13
14	15	16	17	18	19	20
21	22	23	24	25	26	27
28	29	30	31			

☐ January

🌱 FEBRUARY

Sun	Mon	Tue	Wed	Thu	Fri	Sat
				1	2	3
4	5	6	7	8	9	10
11	12	13	14	15	16	17
18	19	20	21	22	23	24
25	26	27	28			

☐ February

🌱 MARCH

Sun	Mon	Tue	Wed	Thu	Fri	Sat
				1	2	3
4	5	6	7	8	9	10
11	12	13	14	15	16	17
18	19	20	21	22	23	24
25	26	27	28	29	30	31

☐ March

☀ MAY

Sun	Mon	Tue	Wed	Thu	Fri	Sat
		1	2	3	4	5
6	7	8	9	10	11	12
13	14	15	16	17	18	19
20	21	22	23	24	25	26
27	28	29	30	31		

☐ May

☀ JUNE

Sun	Mon	Tue	Wed	Thu	Fri	Sat
					1	2
3	4	5	6	7	8	9
10	11	12	13	14	15	16
17	18	19	20	21	22	23
24	25	26	27	28	29	30

☐ June

☀ JULY

Sun	Mon	Tue	Wed	Thu	Fri	Sat
1	2	3	4	5	6	7
8	9	10	11	12	13	14
15	16	17	18	19	20	21
22	23	24	25	26	27	28
29	30	31				

☐ July

🍁 SEPTEMBER

Sun	Mon	Tue	Wed	Thu	Fri	Sat
						1
2	3	4	5	6	7	8
9	10	11	12	13	14	15
16	17	18	19	20	21	22
23	24	25	26	27	28	29
30						

☐ September

🍁 OCTOBER

Sun	Mon	Tue	Wed	Thu	Fri	Sat
	1	2	3	4	5	6
7	8	9	10	11	12	13
14	15	16	17	18	19	20
21	22	23	24	25	26	27
28	29	30	31			

☐ October

❄ NOVEMBER

Sun	Mon	Tue	Wed	Thu	Fri	Sat
				1	2	3
4	5	6	7	8	9	10
11	12	13	14	15	16	17
18	19	20	21	22	23	24
25	26	27	28	29	30	

☐ November

Happy Fool's Day

APRIL

Sun	Mon	Tue	Wed	Thu	Fri	Sat
1	2	3	4	5	6	7
8	9	10	11	12	13	14
15	16	17	18	19	20	21
22	23	24	25	26	27	28
29	30					

☐ April

AUGUST

Sun	Mon	Tue	Wed	Thu	Fri	Sat
			1	2	3	4
5	6	7	8	9	10	11
12	13	14	15	16	17	18
19	20	21	22	23	24	25
26	27	28	29	30	31	

☐ August

DECEMBER

Sun	Mon	Tue	Wed	Thu	Fri	Sat
						1
2	3	4	5	6	7	8
9	10	11	12	13	14	15
16	17	18	19	20	21	22
23	24	25	26	27	28	29
30	31					

☐ December

SET IN MOTION

A *Listen and repeat.* CD 1-40

1. 5/1 May first
2. 5/2 May second
3. 5/3 May third
4. 5/4 May fourth
5. 5/5 May fifth
6. 5/9 May ninth
7. 5/12 May twelfth
8. 5/15 May fifteenth
9. 5/20 May twentieth
10. 5/21 May twenty-first
11. 5/22 May twenty-second
12. 5/23 May twenty-third
13. 5/30 May thirtieth
14. 5/31 May thirty-first

B *Role-play with a partner. Use the vocabulary you have learned.*

Ⓐ When is your birthday?

Ⓑ My birthday is on _____. How about you?

Ⓐ My birthday is on _____.

C *Fill in the blanks with words you have learned.*

① _____ is the third month of the year.

② _____ is the eighth month of the year.

③ Christmas is in _____.

④ New Year's Day is in _____.

⑤ We celebrate Mother's Day in _____.

⑥ _____ comes after May.

⑦ _____ comes before October.

Happy Holidays

61

What Were You Doing?

A *Watch the video clip and check the correct answers.* WEB動画

1. What was Nick doing at three p.m. on March 31?
   ☐ **a.** He was studying.
   ☐ **b.** He was working.
   ☐ **c.** He was cooking.

2. Where was Nick at four a.m. on April 5?
   ☐ **a.** He was at the bank.
   ☐ **b.** He was in bed.
   ☐ **c.** He was in the kitchen.

3. What was Nick doing when Roy called?
   ☐ **a.** He was reading.
   ☐ **b.** He was exercising.
   ☐ **c.** He was watching TV.

4. Why did Roy call Nick?
   ☐ **a.** He wanted to know what Nick was doing.
   ☐ **b.** He wanted to ask Nick for a little help.
   ☐ **c.** He wanted to play a practical joke on Nick.

B *Listen to the conversation and fill in the blanks.* 🎧 1-41 💻

Roy calls his friend Nick and plays a joke on him.

Nick: Hello?

Roy: Hello. This is the police. My name is Officer Tate.

Nick: The police! Are you sure you have the right ¹_____?

Roy: Yes, I am. I'd like to speak to Nick Jenkins.

Nick: ²_____. This is Nick Jenkins. What can I do for you, Officer?

Roy: What were you doing on Tuesday, March 31, at three p.m.?

Nick: Um, I think I was at work. So I was ³_____.

Roy: I see. And what were you doing on April 5 at four a.m.?

Nick: At four a.m.? I was in ⁴_____, of course. I was sleeping.

Roy: Are you sure? Someone ⁵_____ a bank at four a.m.

Nick: It wasn't me. I was sleeping. I'm telling the truth!

Roy: Well, what were you doing when I called? Were you ⁶_____ all the money?

Nick: No, I was ⁷_____. Wait a minute! I know your ⁸_____. Is this Roy?!

Roy: Ha! I got you!

C *Practice the conversation with your partner.*

D *Listen to the conversation and fill in the blanks with the correct month.* 🎧 1-42

Rick

 bowling
February

 watching TV
_____

 reading a book
_____

 playing video games
_____

We use the past continuous tense to describe an action that was happening during a period of time in the past.

> **S. + was/were + V-ing**

This afternoon

Her piano lesson began at three o'clock.

Right now

It's 7:00 now.
Kitty is at home.
She's listening to music.

> She **was playing** the piano then.

Yes/No Questions

Question	"Yes" Response	"No" Response
Was your father **working** at nine o'clock last night?	Yes, he **was working** overtime.	No, he was at home.

Wh- Questions

Question	Response
What **were** you **doing** then?	We **were watching** a movie.

Work It Out

A *Rewrite the sentences using the past continuous tense.*

① I sleep.
  I was sleeping.

② Alex cooks dinner.

③ I write in my diary.

④ Dad and Mom watch TV.

B *Answer the questions based on the hints given.*

① Was he playing baseball? (No / read)
  No, he wasn't. He was reading.

② Were you doing your homework at eight o'clock last night? (Yes)

③ Was Linda surfing the Internet at three o'clock yesterday afternoon? (No / study)

④ Was Matt riding his bike at seven o'clock yesterday morning? (No / sleep)

GRAMMAR | 2 Past Continuous + When + Past Simple

S. + was/were + V-ing + when + S. + V-ed

I began watching TV.

The telephone rang.

3:00 p.m.　　　　4:00 p.m.　　　　5:00 p.m.

I was watching TV.

I was watching TV **when the telephone rang.**

Yes/No Questions

Question	"Yes" Response	"No" Response
Were you studying **when the telephone rang?**	Yes, I was.	No, I was taking a bath.

Wh- Questions

Question	Response
What were they doing **when you saw them?**	They were playing basketball.
What were you doing **when I called you?**	I was sleeping.

Work It Out

A *Fill in the blanks based on the hints given.*

1. A: What _____ you doing when Max _____ (call) you?

   B: I was _____ (chat) with my friend.

2. A: What _____ your mother doing when you _____ (come) back last night?

   B: She _____ _____ (watch) TV.

3. A: What _____ Jeff doing when you _____ (see) him?

   B: He _____ _____ (talk) on the phone.

B *Answer the questions in complete sentences based on the hints given.*

① What was Beth doing when you saw her? (talk on the phone)

   <u>She was talking on the phone.</u>

② What were you doing when it started to rain? (we / shop)

   _____

③ What was Dad doing when Mom called him last night? (work)

   _____

④ What was Jack doing when his mother came home? (do his homework)

   _____

65

This was Helen's summer camp schedule. She had to get up early from Monday to Friday. Her parents hoped she could meet people and be more independent. 🎧 1-43

July

July 15 — 21

	Mon.	Tue.	Wed.	Thur.	Fri.	Sat.	Sun.
9:00 — 10:30	Swimming	Jogging 10 miles	Swimming	Jogging 10 miles	Swimming	✗	City Zoo
10:30 — 11:00	Break					✗	
11:00 — 12:00	Reading	Barbecue	Reading	Barbecue	Reading	✗	
12:00 — 2:00	Lunchtime					✗	
2:00 — 3:30	Tennis	English Lesson	Volleyball	English Lesson	Table Tennis	City Mall	
3:30 — 4:00	Break						
4:00 — 5:00	Boating	Cleaning Time	Boating	Cleaning Time	Boating		
5:00 — 7:00	Dinnertime					✗	✗
7:00 — 9:00	Movie Time	Campfire Story Time	Movie Time	Movie Time	Campfire Story Time	✗	✗
9:00 —	Bedtime						

Ⓐ *Fill in the blanks with the word choices given. Change the word form if necessary.*

> break / mall / mile / jog / independent

1. We drove 250 _____ today.

2. There are plans to build a new _____ in the middle of town.

3. Now that my son is more _____, I have more time for myself.

4. I go _____ every morning.

5. You look really tired. You should take a _____.

Ⓑ *Check the correct answers.*

1. How many times did Helen go boating?
   - ☐ **a.** Once
   - ☐ **b.** Twice
   - ☐ **c.** Three times

2. What was Helen doing from 2:00 p.m. to 3:30 p.m. on Tuesday?
   - ☐ **a.** She was playing tennis.
   - ☐ **b.** She was studying.
   - ☐ **c.** She was boating.

3. When was Helen shopping?
   - ☐ **a.** Friday, July 19, from 7:00 p.m. to 9:00 p.m.
   - ☐ **b.** Saturday, July 20, from 2:00 p.m. to 5:00 p.m.
   - ☐ **c.** Saturday, July 20, from 5:00 p.m. to 9:00 p.m.

4. What did Helen's parents hope?
   - ☐ **a.** That she could do a lot of things by herself
   - ☐ **b.** That she could learn to play a new musical instrument
   - ☐ **c.** That she would always turn to them for help

5. Which is true?
   - ☐ **a.** Her English lesson lasted one hour.
   - ☐ **b.** She had a 30-minute break every two hours.
   - ☐ **c.** She went to the zoo on her last day at the summer camp.

TALKING ABOUT THE TIME

WRITING

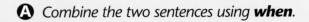

A *Combine the two sentences using **when**.*

① { He was taking a shower.
   The earthquake happened.

He was taking a shower when the earthquake happened.

② { I was playing the piano in my room.
   The phone rang.

_____

③ { They were having a barbecue in the yard.
   I arrived at their house.

_____

④ { We were chatting in the living room.
   My father came home.

_____

B *Jane did a lot of things yesterday. Look at the pictures and write about Jane's day in 50 words.*

1:00–2:00	2:30–3:30	4:00–5:00	6:00–8:00

_____
_____
_____
_____
_____
_____
_____
_____
_____

CHALLENGE YOURSELF

Part I Pictures   1-44

Look at the picture and choose the best answer.

1.

☐ a   ☐ b   ☐ c

2.

☐ a   ☐ b   ☐ c

Part II Question & Response   1-45

Listen to the statement or question and choose the best response.

3. ☐ a   ☐ b   ☐ c   5. ☐ a   ☐ b   ☐ c
4. ☐ a   ☐ b   ☐ c   6. ☐ a   ☐ b   ☐ c

Part III Conversations   1-46

Listen to the conversation and answer the questions.

7. What time is it?
   ☐ a. It's before eight.
   ☐ b. It's eight.
   ☐ c. It's after eight.

8. When is the woman's birthday?
   ☐ a. Her birthday is on May 17.
   ☐ b. Her birthday is on May 13.
   ☐ c. Her birthday is on May 15.

9. What did the woman do?
   ☐ a. She didn't come to the phone.
   ☐ b. She called Stan's house.
   ☐ c. She dialed the wrong number.

10. When is the bank open?
   ☐ a. Only on Saturdays
   ☐ b. The entire week
   ☐ c. Monday through Friday

Linguaporta Training

Let's review the unit with Linguaporta.

Part I   🎧 1-47

Listen to the statement or question and check the best response.

1. ☐ a   ☐ b   ☐ c   3. ☐ a   ☐ b   ☐ c
2. ☐ a   ☐ b   ☐ c   4. ☐ a   ☐ b   ☐ c

Part II   🎧 1-48

Listen to the conversation and check the correct answer.

1. What does the woman say about the soup?
   - ☐ a. It tastes bitter.
   - ☐ b. It's too sweet.
   - ☐ c. It tastes good.

2. How does the man feel?
   - ☐ a. Shy
   - ☐ b. Excited
   - ☐ c. Nervous

3. How does Tommy's mom feel about his test score?
   - ☐ a. She's very nervous.
   - ☐ b. She's very angry.
   - ☐ c. She's very happy.

4. What do the firecrackers do?
   - ☐ a. Scare away evil spirits
   - ☐ b. Bring good luck
   - ☐ c. Welcome the New Year

Part III   🎧 1-49

Listen to the short passage and check the correct picture.

1.

 ☐ a    ☐ b   ☐ c

2.

 ☐ a   ■ b    ☐ c

Part IV

Fill in the blanks.

career / notice / focusing / surprised / date / gift / understand / pleased / envelope / perfect

1. Tim started his _____ as an English teacher last year.
2. Jerome opened the _____ and read the letter.
3. Did you _____ Jack leaving the party early?
4. Matt and I are going on a(n) _____ tonight.
5. Rachel didn't _____ the teacher's question.
6. Nancy is _____ on her history paper.
7. These earrings are a(n) _____ for Jenny.
8. Jennifer is the _____ person for the role.
9. The smart student was _____ that he failed the test.
10. I'm very _____ with my new house.

Part V

Check the correct answer.

1. The movie was boring, _____ I went to sleep.
   ☐ **a.** so ☐ **b.** but ☐ **c.** because ☐ **d.** when

2. Ella was very mad _____ someone stole her purse.
   ☐ **a.** so ☐ **b.** but ☐ **c.** because ☐ **d.** when

3. Oliver _____ eats fast food because he thinks it's unhealthy.
   ☐ **a.** seldom ☐ **b.** always ☐ **c.** often ☐ **d.** almost

4. What were you _____ last night?
   ☐ **a.** do ☐ **b.** did ☐ **c.** to do ☐ **d.** doing

5. I _____ a great movie last night.
   ☐ **a.** am watching ☐ **b.** watch ☐ **c.** watched ☐ **d.** watching

6. Regina goes _____ in the park every morning.
   ☐ **a.** jog ☐ **b.** jogging ☐ **c.** jogs ☐ **d.** to jog

7. My father usually goes to work _____ foot.
   ☐ **a.** with ☐ **b.** of ☐ **c.** on ☐ **d.** by

8. We hope _____ you again.
   ☐ **a.** to see ☐ **b.** seeing ☐ **c.** see ☐ **d.** to seeing

9. I'm so tired. I _____ go to bed now.
   ☐ **a.** want ☐ **b.** am wanting ☐ **c.** am wanting to ☐ **d.** want to

10. I'm thinking about _____ abroad.
    ☐ **a.** study ☐ **b.** studying ☐ **c.** to study ☐ **d.** studied

Read the article and check the correct answer.

"OMG! LOL!" Do you understand those expressions? In the United States, young people are using them more and more. "OMG" is short for "Oh my God!" "LOL" stands for "laughing out loud." For example, if you

5 hear a joke, you might say "LOL!" When something surprises you, you can say "OMG." All of this comes from text messaging. When people send messages, it takes a long time to type "I love you." Some people would rather type "ILY." Instead of "I'll be right back," some people prefer "BRB." Things are changing. Before, people only typed these words. Now, some young Americans are saying them aloud, too.

10 Some adults worry about the changes in English. Experts say that if we always shorten our words, we may decrease the quality of language. However, other people argue that language changes all the time, so there's nothing to worry about. This new language is becoming more complex every day. You might figure out that "TMRW" indicates "tomorrow." But what about "TFTH"? It means "Thanks for the help." You'll never guess what "NALOPKT" means. It stands for

15 "Not a lot of people know that." Some parents say that they can't even talk to their kids anymore! This fad may die out in the future, but who knows? Maybe some day, your grandchildren will say "LYCYLBB." It means, "Love you. See you later. Bye-bye."

1. What is the main topic of the article?
☐ **a.** The difference between children and adults
☐ **b.** The decrease in the quality of language
☐ **c.** A new trend in language

2. What do expressions such as OMG and LOL come from?
☐ **a.** A traditional style of typing
☐ **b.** Text messaging
☐ **c.** Sign language

3. Which is similar in meaning to "I'll come back soon"?
☐ **a.** BRB
☐ **b.** TFTH
☐ **c.** TMRW

4. Which is true?
   ☐ **a.** Every expert says shortening words will decrease the quality of language.
   ☐ **b.** "NALOPKT" means that all the people already know that.
   ☐ **c.** Some young Americans say these shortened words aloud.

5. What does this article say about this new trend of shortening words?
   ☐ **a.** It's not clear if the trend will continue.
   ☐ **b.** It will die before long.
   ☐ **c.** It has already gone out of fashion.

Part VII

Answer the questions in complete sentences with the hints given.

1. What did Cathy do in the kitchen? *(wash the dishes)*
   _____

2. Which subject does Jack like, math or biology? *(biology)*
   _____

3. What does Rachel think about the book? *(interesting)*
   _____

4. Why were you late this morning? *(miss the bus)*
   _____

5. What were you doing when Amanda called? *(take a shower)*
   _____

Answer the questions in complete sentences based on your personal information.

1. What do you usually do on the weekend?
   _____

2. What did you do last weekend?
   _____

3. How do you usually go to school?
   _____

4. How do you like your school?
   _____

5. Are you in any clubs?
   _____

WARM UP

PICTURE DICTIONARY

Listen to the sentences. Each sentence is about something from a fast-food restaurant. Write the sentence number in the correct boxes below. 2-01

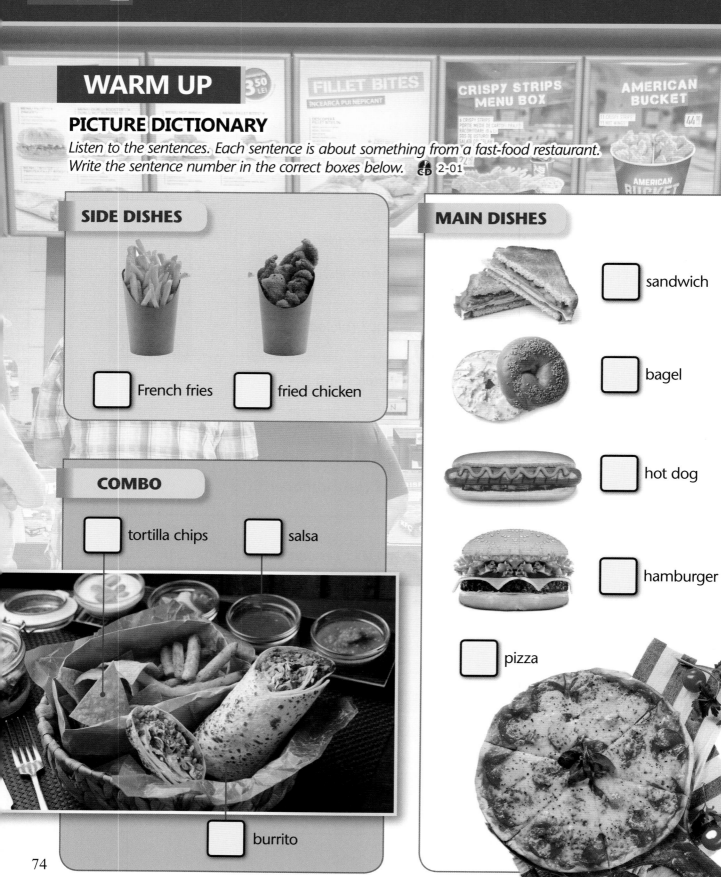

SIDE DISHES

☐ French fries   ☐ fried chicken

COMBO

☐ tortilla chips   ☐ salsa

☐ burrito

MAIN DISHES

☐ sandwich

☐ bagel

☐ hot dog

☐ hamburger

☐ pizza

DESSERT

☐ donut

☐ muffin

☐ waffle

DRINKS

☐ soda   ☐ milkshake

SET IN MOTION

A *Role-play with a partner. Use the vocabulary you have learned.*

Ⓐ What are you going to order?

Ⓑ I'm going to order _____.

....

Ⓐ I'd like a(n) _____.

Ⓑ Is that for here or to go?

....

Ⓐ What would you recommend for _____?

Ⓑ Our _____ is very good. Or you could try the _____.

CONVERSATION

What'll You Have?

A *Watch the video clip and check the correct answers.* WEB動画

1. What is Peter going to order to drink?
   - [ ] **a.** Some soda
   - [ ] **b.** Some coffee
   - [ ] **c.** A milkshake

2. What will Peter do if he isn't full?
   - [ ] **a.** He will order a hot dog.
   - [ ] **b.** He will order another hamburger.
   - [ ] **c.** He will order some more French fries.

3. What is Sharon going to have?
   - [ ] **a.** She's going to have fried chicken.
   - [ ] **b.** She's going to have two hamburgers.
   - [ ] **c.** She's going to have some soda.

4. What does Sharon say to the server?
   - [ ] **a.** She doesn't like her crazy boyfriend.
   - [ ] **b.** Her boyfriend is a bit strange today.
   - [ ] **c.** She doesn't understand what he said.

I'm going to order a super juicy hamburger.

What are you going to order?

B *Listen to the conversation and fill in the blanks.* 🔊 2-02 💻

Sharon and Peter are looking at the menu at a fast-food restaurant.

Sharon: What are you going to order?

Peter: I'm going to order a super juicy hamburger, some super delicious French fries, and a super sweet [1]_____.

Sharon: Boy, you're hungry! Will that be enough for you?

Peter: Yes, it'll be enough. If I'm not [2]_____, I'll order another hamburger.

Sharon: Don't you [3]_____ a juicy hamburger?

Peter: Of course! What are you going to have?

Sharon: I'm going to have some hot [4]_____ chicken.

Peter: Aren't you [5]_____? You should get some super sweet soda!

Sharon: No, thanks. Are you going to talk like that when you order?

Peter: Yes, I am. I'm going to talk like this all day.

Server: Welcome to Super Burger. [6]_____ you have?

Peter: I'll have a super juicy hamburger, please.

Server: Excuse me?

Sharon: Sorry. My boyfriend is a little [7]_____ today.

Server: That's OK. Would you like some super [8]_____ fries to go with it?

C *Practice the conversation with your partner.*

D *The following are adjectives that describe food. Listen to the conversation and write the adjectives with the food.* 🔊 2-03

delicious / bitter / ✓sweet / hot / sour

milkshake
_____sweet_____

coffee
_____

lemonade
_____

fried chicken
_____

cake
_____

GRAMMAR   **1 Future Tense**

The simple future tense refers to an action that happens at a future time.

 Cindy goes to school every day.
She's always there from 8:00 to 4:00.

Past	Present	Future

It was 8:00.
Cindy was at school.

It's 10:00 now.
Cindy is at school.

At 10:00 tomorrow,
she **will be** at school.

Yes/No Questions

Question	"Yes" Response	"No" Response
Will you be at school?	Yes, I **will**.	No, I **won't**. I'll be at home.

Wh- Questions

Question	Response
What **will** you have?	We'll have two hamburgers and some French fries.
Who **will** go to a movie with you?	My boyfriend **will**.

Work It Out

Ⓐ *Answer the questions in complete sentences based on the hints given.*

① Will you study? (No / play the piano)
  No, I won't. I'll play the piano.

② Will you go to the library tomorrow? (No / stay at home)
  _____

③ Where will you be this evening? (at home)
  _____

④ When will the movie start? (in 15 minutes)
  _____

Ⓑ *Write the questions based on the responses and the hints given.*

① *Will you go shopping tomorrow?*
  Yes, I will. (shopping tomorrow)

② _____
  Yes, I will. (play the online game)

③ _____
  No, they won't. (go hiking this weekend)

④ _____
  I'll go to <u>the mall</u> tomorrow.

2 Be Going To

We use "be going to" when a decision is influenced or planned by something or someone.

I'm going to see a movie tonight.

be going to + base verb

Yes/No Questions

Question	"Yes" Response	"No" Response
Are you **going to** do the dishes?	Yes, I am.	No, I'm not. I'**m going to** do my homework.
Is Dad **going to** work tonight?	Yes, he is.	No, he isn't. He'**s going to** eat dinner with us.

Wh- Questions

Question	Response
What **are you going to** order?	I'**m going to** order a hot dog and a soda.
Where **are they going to** eat?	They'**re going to** eat at Pizza Hut.
Why **aren't you going to** go shopping with us?	Because I have to finish this report today. Sorry.

Work It Out

Ⓐ *Write the questions based on the hints given.*

① I'm going to watch TV. (what)(Yes/No question)

    What are you going to do?

    Are you going to watch TV?

② She's going to rent a video. (what)

③ They are going to go camping this weekend. (Yes/No question)

④ My grandparents are going to have dinner with us. (Who)

⑤ Tom is going to go to Korea next year. (Yes/No question)

A World of Restaurants

2-04

Traveling is a lot of fun. You can meet new people, and you can try new food! In Western countries, there are many kinds of restaurants.

Steak Houses

Steak houses are usually expensive. They serve
5 steaks, but they often have seafood, too.
People go to steak houses on special days,
such as birthdays and anniversaries.

Diners

Diners are very popular in the United States.
10 They aren't expensive, and people go there
for breakfast, lunch, and dinner. They usually
serve only one kind of coffee. However, the
server will fill your cup as many times as you
like.

15 ### Fast-Food Restaurants

In Western countries, fast-food restaurants
are everywhere. And they sell more than just
hamburgers and French fries. They sell fish
and chips, Mexican food, hot dogs, Japanese
20 food, and even Chinese food.

Next time you travel, pick your favorite restaurant and try something new!

A *Fill in the blanks with the word choices given. Change the word form if necessary.*

> even / serve / expensive / however / anniversary

1. We celebrated our first wedding _____ in January.
2. Meals can be _____ to you in your room.
3. It's _____ to live in New York.
4. I said hello, but Meg didn't _____ look at me.
5. This is one solution to the problem. _____, there are others.

B *Check the correct answers.*

1. When do people go to steak houses?
   - ☐ **a.** On the weekend
   - ☐ **b.** All the time
   - ☐ **c.** On their anniversary

2. How much does it cost to eat at diners?
   - ☐ **a.** It costs a lot of money.
   - ☐ **b.** It doesn't cost much money.
   - ☐ **c.** It costs more than eating at a steak house.

3. What meals do people eat at diners?
   - ☐ **a.** Lunch and dinner
   - ☐ **b.** Breakfast and lunch
   - ☐ **c.** Breakfast, lunch, and dinner

4. What is true about the coffee at diners?
   - ☐ **a.** It is served in a special cup.
   - ☐ **b.** It is served in the morning.
   - ☐ **c.** There is only one kind available.

5. Where can you find fast-food restaurants in Western countries?
   - ☐ **a.** All over the place
   - ☐ **b.** Near schools and parks
   - ☐ **c.** In poor neighborhoods

UNIT
07

EATING OUT

81

WRITING

A *Fill in the blanks and answer the questions with the hints given.*

① ___Do___ you have any plans on Friday night? *(yes / go to the movies)*

Yes, I'm going to the movies.

② _____ is going to go with you? *(Mike and Sarah)*

_____

③ _____ are you going to get there? *(bus)*

_____

④ _____ will you be home? *(10:30 p.m.)*

_____

B *Write information about your favorite restaurant. Then, use the information you write to complete the sentences below.*

Restaurant name: _____

Type of restaurant:

☐ American ☐ Japanese

☐ Chinese ☐ Mexican

☐ Italian ☐ French

(other) _____

Three menu items:

1. _____

2. _____

3. _____

My favorite food on the menu: _____

_____ is my favorite restaurant. It is a(n) _____

restaurant. I often eat there with _____ (people). My favorite food

there is _____. _____

_____

_____

CHALLENGE YOURSELF

Part I Pictures 2-05

Look at the picture and choose the best answer.

1.

☐ a   ☐ b   ☐ c

2.

☐ a   ☐ b   ☐ c

Part II Question & Response 2-06

Listen to the statement or question and choose the best response.

3. ☐ a   ☐ b   ☐ c   5. ☐ a   ☐ b   ☐ c
4. ☐ a   ☐ b   ☐ c   6. ☐ a   ☐ b   ☐ c

Part III Conversations 2-07

Listen to the conversation and answer the questions.

7. What did the grasshoppers taste like?
   ☐ a. They tasted like fried chicken.
   ☐ b. They tasted like French fries.
   ☐ c. They tasted like ketchup.

8. Who is the man talking to?
   ☐ a. His daughter
   ☐ b. A server
   ☐ c. A customer

9. Why doesn't Trevor want tuna fish?
   ☐ a. He doesn't think it will taste good.
   ☐ b. He's really tired of eating tuna fish.
   ☐ c. He doesn't want to eat cold food.

10. What does the woman want?
    ☐ a. She wants something to drink.
    ☐ b. She wants something to eat.
    ☐ c. She wants something to wear.

Linguaporta Training

Let's review the unit with Linguaporta.

At the Supermarket

WARM UP

PICTURE DICTIONARY

Listen to the sentences. Each sentence is about something from a supermarket.
Write the sentence number in the correct boxes below. CD 2-08

☐ frozen food(s)

☐ canned food(s)

☐ beverage(s)

☐ packaged food(s)

☐ fruit(s)

☐ seafood

☐ dairy product(s)

☐ baked good(s)

☐ meat(s)

☐ vegetable(s)

SET IN MOTION

A *Role-play with a partner. Use the vocabulary you have learned.*

A: Where were you last night?

B: I was at the supermarket.

A: What did you buy there?

B: I bought some _____.

B *Put the words in the box into the correct section.*

ice cream	watermelons
instant noodles	chicken
milk	canned fish
canned beans	cake
clams	apples
beef	corn
shrimps	cheese
soda	bread
tea	cabbages

Frozen Foods

Canned Foods

Beverages

Packaged Foods

Fruit

Seafood

Dairy Products

Baked Goods

Meat

Vegetables

Getting Everything on the List

A *Watch the video clip and check the correct answers.* WEB動画 🖥️

1. Which is NOT on sale?
   - ☐ **a.** Soap
   - ☐ **b.** Eggs
   - ☐ **c.** Shampoo

2. How many eggs do Jim and Wendy want?
   - ☐ **a.** Twelve
   - ☐ **b.** Twenty-four
   - ☐ **c.** Thirty-six

3. What kind of milk do Jim and Wendy want?
   - ☐ **a.** Regular milk
   - ☐ **b.** Non-fat milk
   - ☐ **c.** Low-fat milk

4. In how many days will the milk expire?
   - ☐ **a.** One
   - ☐ **b.** Two
   - ☐ **c.** Three

B *Listen to the conversation and fill in the blanks.* CD 2-09 WEB動画 💻

Wendy and Jim are doing grocery shopping.

Wendy: OK, you grab a cart, and I'll look over these coupons.

Jim: All right, I'm ready. Is there anything good on sale?

Wendy: There are specials on soap, shampoo, and toothbrushes.

Jim: Great. We can get those after we find the stuff on our list. You brought the
¹_____ list, right?

Wendy: Of course. We need to get some milk and eggs. We also need two ²_____ of
bread.

Jim: Milk and eggs are over there in the dairy ³_____. Bread is on the other side
of the store.

Wendy: I'll get the bread. Meet me in the back of the store at the meat section.

Jim: OK. We need two ⁴_____ grade-A eggs and some milk.

Wendy: Remember to get ⁵_____ milk.

Jim: And you remember to get ⁶_____ wheat bread.

Wendy: Did you check the expiration date on those?

Jim: Sorry, I ⁷_____. The eggs are OK, but the milk expires in two days.

Wendy: I think you should get another one. Did you check to see if any of the eggs are
⁸_____?

Jim: They're all fine.

C *Practice the conversation with your partner.*

D *Listen to the three short conversations. What did/do the speakers buy? Match the pictures with the
conversation.* CD 2-10

a   b   c   d

① _____

② _____

e   f   g   h

③ _____

87

GRAMMAR 1 Modal Verbs

Modal Verb	Usage	Example
can, could	ability	Can Fiona play soccer?
	permission	Could I speak to Mr. Smith?
	possibility	Anyone can make mistakes.
may, might	permission	May I sit here?
	possibility	Philip might be sick.
should	advice	You should be more careful.

Can / Be Able To

can / be able to

cannot, can't / be not able to

- Bill **can** swim well.
= Bill **is able to** swim well.

- Luke **cannot** swim well.
= Luke **isn't able to** swim well.

Work It Out

A *Change **can** to **be able to**.*

① Helen and Linda can play tennis.

   Helen and Linda are able to play tennis.

② Tina can speak Spanish well.

___

③ My mother can't swim.

___

④ Can you play hockey?

___

B *Match the sentences.*

① Can I have another piece of cake?   •   • Yes, I'd like a tuna sandwich, please.

② I think I may have a cold.   •   • OK. I will.

③ You should be more careful.   •   • All right. I'll stay at home.

④ May I take your order?   •   • Why don't you take today off?

⑤ You shouldn't go out.   •   • Sure. Help yourself.

88

Countable Nouns

a lot of/lots of **many** (a) few some any	+	bananas eggs cookies hot dogs apples

Uncountable Nouns

a lot of/lots of **much** (a) little some any	+	meat bread soda tea cheese

Countable	Uncountable
Jane buys **some** apples every week.	Jane has **some** money.
Did you buy **any** bananas?	Did you buy **any** soda?
I don't have **many** friends.	I don't have **much** time.
I have **a few** friends.	We have **a little** time.

I eat **an apple** every day.

I eat **rice** every day.

a (something) of + Uncountable Noun

a bowl of rice/soup	a glass of water/juice	a piece of cake/pizza	a bottle of soda/juice
a carton of milk/juice	a cup of coffee/tea	a loaf of bread	

UNIT
08

AT THE SUPERMARKET

Work It Out

A *Check the correct answers.*

① Jeff doesn't drink (☐ much / ☐ many) water during the day.

② Jean bought (☐ a lot of / ☐ a little) tank tops yesterday.

③ I like to eat (☐ any / ☐ some) bread for my breakfast.

④ Do you want to buy (☐ any / ☐ much) beverages?

⑤ Ted eats (☐ a few / ☐ a little) meat, but he eats (☐ plenty of / ☐ much) vegetables.

⑥ How (☐ much / ☐ many) ice cream did you eat?

⑦ How (☐ much / ☐ many) students are there in your class?

B *Fill in the blanks with the words provided. Make changes if necessary.*

loaf / bowl / cup / bottle

① Can I have another _____ of bread?

② Would you like a _____ of coffee?

③ I bought two _____ of soda for his birthday party at the supermarket.

④ Do you want another _____ of rice?

Comewell Supermarket Special Offers

HUGE DISCOUNTS THIS WEEK ONLY !

From April 15 to the 21 at large stores only

Discounted Items:

BILLY's 100% ORANGE JUICE

~~$11~~

NOW ONLY

$9 /each

ABC CHEESE

~~$7/each~~

NOW ONLY

$10 /2

LIVE BREAKFAST CEREAL

~~$19~~

NOW ONLY

$17

JUICY APPLES

~~$3~~

NOW ONLY

$1 /each

GOLDEN FARM CABBAGE

~~$4~~

NOW ONLY

$3 /each

✂- - - - - - - - - - - - - - - -

$2 COUPON

Good for any bottle of soda during this special-offer period

Only one coupon per purchase. Cannot be used with any other special offer.

MANY ITEMS 10% OFF!

Look for items with the special Smiley Face.

- Buy any loaf of whole wheat bread and get another for half price.

  (*This offer does not include Wendel's Whole Wheat Bread.*)

- With all these great special offers, you're certain to leave Comewell with lots of big, heavy bags. Be sure to take advantage of our FREE DELIVERY service.

  (*On purchases over $150. Delivery within the city only.*)

A *Fill in the blanks with the word choices given. Change the word form if necessary.*

> huge / item / each / delivery / include

1. Does the price _____ tax?

2. We offer free home _____ on orders over $300.

3. Jane lives in a(n) _____ house.

4. This _____ is on sale.

5. Ms. Kane gave _____ of the children a gift.

B *Check the correct answers.*

1. When do the special offers start?
   - ☐ **a.** April 15
   - ☐ **b.** April 21
   - ☐ **c.** It doesn't say.

2. How much will a $10 box of cookies cost if it has the special Smiley Face?
   - ☐ **a.** $9
   - ☐ **b.** $15
   - ☐ **c.** $1

3. How much will two loaves of $15 Wendel's Whole Wheat Bread now cost?
   - ☐ **a.** $15
   - ☐ **b.** $22
   - ☐ **c.** $30

4. If you live in the city and spend $220 on groceries at Comewell Supermarket, how much will you need to pay to have them delivered to your home?
   - ☐ **a.** Nothing
   - ☐ **b.** $70
   - ☐ **c.** $150

5. How much will you pay for a $35 bottle of Comewell soda if you have two coupons?
   - ☐ **a.** $28
   - ☐ **b.** $31
   - ☐ **c.** $33

WRITING

A *Fanny's Grocery Store, Uncle Liao's Corner Store and Reya's Supermarket are all nearby. Check out their prices and answer the questions.*

Fanny's Grocery Store

chocolate
$3 *a bar*
$9 *for a pack of four bars*

soda
$3 *a can*
$15 *for a six-pack of soda*

chips
$3 *a pack*

Uncle Liao's Corner Store

chocolate
$3 *a bar*

soda
$3 *a can*

chips
$4 *a pack*

Reya's Supermarket

chocolate
$3 *a bar*
$4 *for two*

soda
$3 *a can*
$16 *for a six-pack of soda*

chips
$3 *a pack*
$28 *for 10 packs*

① Which store has the most expensive chips?

_____

② Andrew wants to buy four chocolate bars. Which store has the lowest price?

_____

③ If you want to buy six cans of soda, which store has the cheapest price?

_____

④ How much do 10 packs of chips cost at Uncle Liao's Corner Store?

_____

B *Make a shopping list and write a short passage about what you're going to buy in 50 words.*

SHOPPING LIST	
☐	_____
☐	_____
☐	_____
☐	_____
☐	_____
☐	_____

CHALLENGE YOURSELF

Part I Pictures ● CD 2-12

Look at the picture and choose the best answer.

1.

☐ a   ☐ b   ☐ c

2.

☐ a   ☐ b   ☐ c

Part II Question & Response ● CD 2-13

Listen to the statement or question and choose the best response.

3. ☐ a   ☐ b   ☐ c   5. ☐ a   ☐ b   ☐ c
4. ☐ a   ☐ b   ☐ c   6. ☐ a   ☐ b   ☐ c

Part III Conversations ● CD 2-14

Listen to the conversation and answer the questions.

7. What does Marty want?
   ☐ a. Canned foods
   ☐ b. Dairy products
   ☐ c. Baked goods

8. What does the customer have to do if she wants a discount?
   ☐ a. She has to have a coupon.
   ☐ b. She has to take a flight.
   ☐ c. She has to come back next week.

9. Which of the following is true?
   ☐ a. Scipio's Pizza always has free delivery.
   ☐ b. Scipio's Pizza has free delivery for an order of two pizzas.
   ☐ c. Scipio's Pizza offers two pizzas for the price of one.

10. How much will the customer spend on beverages?
    ☐ a. $9
    ☐ b. $2
    ☐ c. $4

Linguaporta Training

Let's review the unit with Linguaporta.

Hobbies

WARM UP

PICTURE DICTIONARY

Listen to the dialogues. Each dialogue is about a different hobby. Write the dialogue number in the correct boxes below. 🎧 2-15

[ ] paint pictures

[ ] go hiking

[ ] play cards

[ ] take photos

[ ] listen to music

[ ] play pool

[ ] go rock climbing

[ ] go fishing

[ ] go camping

go cycling

collect coins

play video games

SET IN MOTION

A *Role-play with a partner. Use the vocabulary you have learned.*

(A) Where were you yesterday?

(B) I was with friends.

(A) What did you do?

(B) I _____ .

B *Do you know what hobbies are outdoor activities and what hobbies are indoor activities? Maybe some hobbies can be both. Write them in the correct space.*

Outdoor Activities

_____

_____

_____

Indoor Activities

_____

_____

_____

Outdoor or Indoor Activities

paint pictures

_____

_____

Your Hobbies

_____

_____

_____

Exploring New Hobbies

A *Watch the video clip and check the correct answers.* WEB動画 🖥️📱

1. Which sport did Carol mention that she enjoyed playing?
- ☐ **a.** Soccer
- ☐ **b.** Baseball
- ☐ **c.** Tennis

2. What is Sam's idea of fun?
- ☐ **a.** Going hiking
- ☐ **b.** Reading books
- ☐ **c.** Writing poems

3. Why does Carol like to do sports?
- ☐ **a.** It helps her lose weight.
- ☐ **b.** It lets her relieve stress.
- ☐ **c.** It allows her to escape from the world.

4. What are they going to do?
- ☐ **a.** Try one of the other's hobbies
- ☐ **b.** Go to another restaurant
- ☐ **c.** Talk about their favorite movie

So, what are your interests?

Well, I'm into all kinds of sports.

B *Listen to the conversation and fill in the blanks.* 🎵 2-16 📺

Carol and Sam are on a first date at a restaurant, and they are getting to know each other better.

Sam: So, what are your interests?

Carol: Well, I'm ^{1}_____ all kinds of sports. I play basketball at school, and I play soccer with friends on the weekend.

Sam: I'm not really ^{2}_____ at sports.

Carol: Oh, but I have various other ^{3}_____. I also bicycle for fun, and sometimes I go hiking.

Sam: It ^{4}_____ like you enjoy the outdoors.

Carol: I do. What about you? What do you do in your free time?

Sam: I like to ^{5}_____ and paint. I also enjoy reading. That's my idea of fun.

Carol: I think I get enough reading at school. What's so much fun about that?

Sam: Well, reading is ^{6}_____, and it lets me escape from the world for a little bit.

Carol: I can relate to that. But I don't think I'd like sitting still for that long. I like sports because they're great for relieving ^{7}_____.

Sam: It sounds pretty tiring.

Carol: No, really. How about this? I'll try one of your hobbies if you'll try one of ^{8}_____.

Sam: You're on.

C *Practice the conversation with your partner.*

D *Listen to the short conversation. What is mentioned in the conversation? Check the correct pictures.*

🎵 2-17

☐    ☐    ☐    ☐

*Most verbs are **action verbs**. They tell what the subject does. Some verbs link an adjective or a noun to the subject. We call them **linking verbs**. They include: be, become, feel, get, look, taste, smell, sound, and turn.*

Sense Verbs

$$\text{S. + look/feel/taste/smell/sound +} \begin{cases} \textbf{like + N.} \\ \textbf{adj.} \end{cases}$$

- Ginny's eyes **look like** her mother's.
- The milk in the refrigerator **smells** funny.

be/become/get/turn

$$\text{S. + be/become/get/turn +} \begin{cases} \textbf{N.} \\ \textbf{adj.} \end{cases}$$

- I want to become a good dancer.
- Carol gets tired easily these days.
- I'd like to get married before I turn 30.

*Some linking verbs can be used in more than one way. Action verbs are usually used with **adverbs**, not **adjectives**.*

Example Sentence	Verb Usage	Meaning
Her face **turned** red with anger.	linking verb	to change
The road **turns** sharply.	action verb	to curve

Work It Out

Ⓐ *Check the correct answers.*

① The fruit (☐ looks / ☐ looks like) an orange, but it's definitely not one.

② This song (☐ sounds / ☐ sounds like) another song I recently heard.

③ The child's cheeks (☐ feel / ☐ feel like) hot because he has a fever.

④ Your house (☐ looks / ☐ looks like) wonderful! How long did it take you to decorate it?

⑤ A: This doesn't (☐ look / ☐ look like) an apple at all.

   B: I never said it was an apple. I did say, though, that it (☐ tasted / ☐ tasted like) one.

Ⓑ *Check the correct answers.*

① Frank got (☐ angry / ☐ angrily) and left the room.

② An old woman appeared (☐ sudden / ☐ suddenly) in front of me.

③ Everything is all right. Just stay (☐ calm / ☐ calmly).

④ They lived (☐ happy / ☐ happily) ever after.

⑤ Could you speak more (☐ slow / ☐ slowly)?

2 Possessive Pronouns

It's mine.

This seat is <u>my seat</u>, not <u>your seat</u>.

➡ This seat is **mine**, not **yours**.

Subject	Possessive Adjective	Possessive Pronoun
I	my	mine
we	our	ours
you	your	yours
he	his	his
she	her	hers
it	its	its
they	their	theirs

A: Whose book <u>is</u> this?

B: It's <u>his</u>.
    └➤ = his book

A: Whose books <u>are</u> these?

B: They're <u>mine</u>.
    └➤ = my books

a friend of mine, friends of mine
- Are those people friends of yours?
- I went to a movie with a friend of mine.

UNIT
09

HOBBIES

Work It Out

A *Fill in the blanks.*

① My car is red, and his car is blue. = My car is red and _____ is blue.

② Some of the paintings are our paintings. = Some of the paintings are _____.

③ These are my kids. Where are your kids? = These are my kids. Where are _____?

④ This is our house, and that is their house. = This is our house, and that is _____.

⑤ My earrings are small, but her earrings are big.
= My earrings are small, but _____ are big.

B *Check the correct answers.*

① This is a pretty hat. Is it (☐ your / ☐ yours)?

② My hair is longer than (☐ her / ☐ hers).

③ Can I use your cell phone? I forgot to bring (☐ my / ☐ mine).

④ That's not my bag. (☐ My / ☐ Mine) bag is red.

⑤ I didn't have a pencil, so Mandy gave me (☐ her / ☐ hers).

Parkour:
The Art of Movement

🎧 2-18

People are jumping, rolling, and swinging their way across cities all over the world. Who are they? These people are parkour athletes! Parkour is a sport that has turned normal cities into <u>obstacle</u> courses. The idea of parkour is simple. Start at one location and move to another location—but move as quickly as you can.
5 In order to move faster, you have to use objects in your path to help you. For example, instead of running around a wall, climb over it! Do anything you can to keep moving forward.

Though parkour looks exciting, it can be very dangerous. To practice parkour safely, you must train carefully to build up strength, balance, and coordination.
10 Thankfully, there are communities all around the world that help people learn parkour.

Do you think parkour sounds fun? You're in luck! Since parkour is more popular than ever, there are plenty of groups you can join. With training, you can become more confident and show your moves to the world. Best of all, you'll get to
15 experience the sense of freedom that only comes from parkour!

Ⓐ *Fill in the blanks with the word choices given. Change the word form if necessary.*

> **path / simple / instead of / confident / object**

1. I'm _____ that we can win this game.
2. Could I have soda _____ coffee?
3. Two men blocked my _____, so I couldn't move forward.
4. We could see a moving _____ in the sky.
5. That's a(n) _____ math problem, but I didn't understand it.

Ⓑ *Check the correct answers.*

1. The underlined word "obstacle" means an object which _____ your way.
   - ☐ **a.** finds
   - ☐ **b.** makes
   - ☐ **c.** blocks

2. How would a parkour athlete get past a wall?
   - ☐ **a.** Run around it
   - ☐ **b.** Climb over it
   - ☐ **c.** Break through it

3. What is the goal of parkour?
   - ☐ **a.** To move slowly and carefully
   - ☐ **b.** To move as quickly as possible
   - ☐ **c.** To move dangerously

4. How can you practice parkour safely?
   - ☐ **a.** Try parkour right away without practicing
   - ☐ **b.** Spend a long time training and learning
   - ☐ **c.** There is no way to practice parkour safely.

5. Which of the following is true?
   - ☐ **a.** Parkour used to be more popular all over the world.
   - ☐ **b.** There are only a few communities where you can learn parkour.
   - ☐ **c.** Building up strength, balance and coordination is important to parkour.

A *Write sentences using the following linking verbs.*

① sound

_____

② look

_____

③ taste

_____

④ smell

_____

B *Please answer all questions honestly and thoroughly.*

① How often do you participate in sport or physical activity?

☐ Daily   ☐ Weekly   ☐ Monthly   ☐ Yearly   ☐ Never

② How many hours a week, on average, do you participate in sports or physical activity?

☐ 0-1 hour   ☐ 1-2 hours   ☐ 2-4 hours   ☐ 4+ hours

③ Please state what sport you do at school.

_____
_____
_____
_____

④ Where do you normally buy your sports clothing and equipment? How much do you spend on sports clothing and equipment?

_____
_____
_____
_____
_____

Part I Pictures CD 2-19

Look at the picture and choose the best answer.

1.

□ a   □ b   □ c

2.

□ a   □ b   □ c

Part II Question & Response CD 2-20

Listen to the statement or question and choose the best response.

3. □ a   □ b   □ c   **5.** □ a   □ b   □ c

4. □ a   □ b   □ c   **6.** □ a   □ b   □ c

Part III Conversations CD 2-21

Listen to the conversation and answer the questions.

7. What did the man and woman do yesterday?
 □ a. They went cycling.
 □ b. They went fishing.
 □ c. They went hiking.

8. What does the man think about what Amy said?
 □ a. He thinks it was very funny.
 □ b. He thinks she just went bowling.
 □ c. He thinks she didn't tell the truth.

9. What did the woman think of the movie?
 □ a. She thought it was very good.
 □ b. She thought it was terrible.
 □ c. She thought it was too long.

10. What does the man say about painting?
 □ a. He does it for fun.
 □ b. He's new at doing it.
 □ c. He does it to make money.

Linguaporta Training

Let's review the unit with Linguaporta.

UNIT
09

HOBBIES

WARM UP

PICTURE DICTIONARY

Listen to the sentences. Each sentence is about a different item from a clothing store. Write the sentence number in the correct boxes below. 🎧 2-22

KEY ITEMS

lace dress

one-piece swimsuit

TOPS

shirt

sweater

tank top

jacket

ACCESSORIES

sunglasses

earrings

coat

polo shirt

BOTTOMS

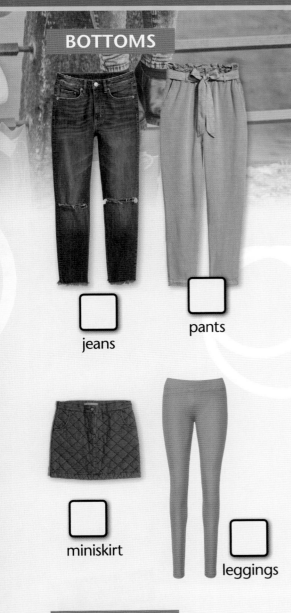

jeans

pants

miniskirt

leggings

SHOES

sneakers

high heels

boots

SET IN MOTION

Ⓐ *Role-play with a partner. Use the vocabulary you have learned.*

Ⓐ How much do/does the _____ cost?

Ⓑ It costs / They cost _____.

....

Ⓐ What's the material of this _____?

Ⓑ It's made of _____.

Ⓑ *Listen to the conversation and fill in the blanks.* 🎧 2-23

Oliver: I like this one, but it's a _____. I only wear _____ shirts.

Eliza: Let's ask the clerk if they have it in your _____.

Oliver: Excuse me, do you have this in medium?

Clerk: Let me check the storeroom to see if we have any _____. Please wait a moment.

Eliza: That would be great, thank you!

Clerk: You're in luck, sir! This is the last medium we have in this _____.

Finding the Right Fit

A *Watch the video clip and check the correct answers.* WEB動画 🖥️

1. What is Denis interested in finding?
- ☐ **a.** Biking shorts
- ☐ **b.** Hiking boots
- ☐ **c.** Exercise pants

2. Which color is out of stock?
- ☐ **a.** Red
- ☐ **b.** Pink
- ☐ **c.** Blue

3. How much are the blue pants?
- ☐ **a.** $10
- ☐ **b.** $15
- ☐ **c.** $50

4. What is wrong with the clothes Denis tries on?
- ☐ **a.** They are made for women.
- ☐ **b.** They are too small.
- ☐ **c.** They are too big.

They're $10.

How much do they cost?

106

B *Listen to the conversation and fill in the blanks.* 🎧 2-24 🖥️

Salesperson: Hello. Can I help you find anything?

Denis: Actually, I was interested in some pants to [1]_____ in. Do you have anything like that?

Salesperson: Of course. We have [2]_____ different styles. They're right this way.

Denis: Wow! These are cool. Do they come in any other [3]_____?

Salesperson: The brown and pink pants are very popular, but we're out of [4]_____ right now.

Denis: Oh, well, I guess blue is OK. How much do they [5]_____?

Salesperson: They're $10.

Denis: Where can I try these on?

Salesperson: The [6]_____ rooms are in the back of the store.

Denis: Thanks.

Salesperson: Is everything all right in there?

Denis: Um, I'm not sure these are the [7]_____ size.

Salesperson: Why don't I get a [8]_____ size for you? How about a size six?

Denis: I think that's a good idea. Thanks.

C *Practice the conversation with your partner.*

D *Listen to the three short conversations. Check the correct pictures.* 🎧 2-25

① ☐   ☐

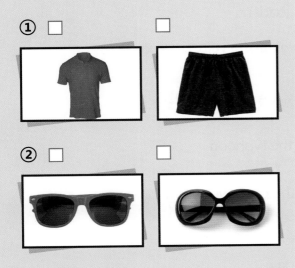

② ☐   ☐

③ ☐   ☐

UNIT
10

SHOP TILL YOU DROP

107

Active Voice VS. Passive Voice

| S. + be + p.p + (by somebody) |

Active Dave made our club's website.
         S.   V.   O.

Passive Our club's website was made by Dave.
                           be + p.p.

When to Use

Passive voice is used when the focus is on the action. It's not important to know who or what does the action.

• My passport <u>was stolen</u>.
  → *We don't know who did the action.*

• The classrooms <u>are cleaned</u> every day by students.
  → *Students are not important here, and the word can be removed.*

• Instagram <u>is used</u> by people around the world.
  → *We want to focus more on Instagram than people around the world.*

Work It Out

Ⓐ *Check the correct answers.*

① Soccer (☐ plays / ☐ is played) in many countries.

② The president (☐ made / ☐ was made) the final decision.

③ Tina and Beth (☐ invited / ☐ were invited) to the party, but they didn't go.

④ Beethoven (☐ composed / ☐ was composed) the music.

⑤ The driver (☐ killed / ☐ was killed) in the accident.

Ⓑ *Change all the following **active voice** sentences into **passive voice** sentences.*

① A.A. Milne wrote *Winnie-the-Pooh* in 1926.

   Winnie-the-Pooh _____ by A.A. Milne in 1926.

② The typhoon caused great damage.

   Great damage _____ by the typhoon.

③ The police found the stolen car yesterday.

   The stolen car _____ by the police yesterday.

④ A famous writer will give a speech after dinner.

   A speech _____ by a famous writer after dinner.

⑤ Chuck has to finish the work before next Friday.

   The work _____ by Chuck before next Friday.

Money

> **Thing + cost + (person) + money**

$20

$50

$250

- The train ticket **costs** $20.
- Three sweaters only **cost** $50.
- The pair of jeans **cost** me $250.

> The total is $320.

> **Person + spend + money +** { **on N.** / **V-ing** }

- I **spend** $300 **on** my clothes each month.
- She **spends** $6 **on** the train every day.
- We only **spent** $20 **eating** at the diner yesterday.

Time

> **It + take + (person) + time + to V.**

- It **takes** me an hour **to get** to work every morning.
- It **took** him 20 minutes **to walk** to the train station.

> **Person + spend + time +** { **on N.** / **V-ing** }

- He **spends** two hours **playing** online games every day.
- We **spent** a whole month **on** the new project.
- They **spent** two hours **studying** last night.

Work It Out

A *Check the correct answers.*

① My new jacket (☐ spent / ☐ cost / ☐ took) me $300.

② I (☐ spent / ☐ cost / ☐ took) $300 on my new jacket.

③ I (☐ spent / ☐ cost / ☐ took) two hours looking for a new jacket.

④ It (☐ spent / ☐ cost / ☐ took) me two hours to find the jacket I wanted.

⑤ My mother thinks I (☐ spend / ☐ cost / ☐ take) too much time and money shopping for clothes, but I don't agree.

⑥ Jack (☐ spends / ☐ costs / ☐ takes) a lot of money (☐ in / ☐ on / ☐ with) computer games.

Online Shopping Catches On

🎧 2-26

As technology gets better, more and more people are connecting to the Internet to shop online. Shopping online is usually quicker and often costs less money. People value their time and money, so it's not surprising that customers are changing their ways.

5   One popular kind of shopping site is the Internet auction. Here, people can buy and sell almost anything, including clothes and accessories. There are even cars, computers, and homes for sale. At first, these sites were used by people hoping to sell off unwanted items. Now, those same sellers have become business people. They use Internet auctions to make a living. Some of them are growing rich from
10 their online stores.

Internet auctions are very popular among university students. As well as using the sites for bargain hunting, some run their own online retail businesses after class. Art students use Internet auctions as a way to present their own work to the public and view the latest trends in the field. Everyone can benefit from online shopping!

A *Fill in the blanks with the word choices given. Change the word form if necessary.*

> clothes / customer / latest / including / field

1. Have you seen his _____ movie?
2. Ten people, _____ two children, were injured in the accident.
3. Jeff was a pioneer in the _____ of digital art.
4. Mr. Smith is one of our regular _____.
5. Carol usually wears casual _____.

B *Check the correct answers.*

1. Which is NOT mentioned as a reason for online shopping becoming more popular?
   - ☐ **a.** Technology is really improving.
   - ☐ **b.** Online shopping is cheaper.
   - ☐ **c.** Stores are too crowded.

2. What do business people use Internet auctions for?
   - ☐ **a.** To meet people
   - ☐ **b.** To earn money
   - ☐ **c.** To research

3. What were Internet auction sites first used for?
   - ☐ **a.** To sell unwanted things
   - ☐ **b.** To sell new clothes and accessories
   - ☐ **c.** To buy and sell currency

4. Which is true?
   - ☐ **a.** Art students hardly use Internet auctions.
   - ☐ **b.** Internet auctions aren't popular among college students.
   - ☐ **c.** People can buy houses online.

5. What is another suitable title for this article?
   - ☐ **a.** Business People Moving to the U.S.
   - ☐ **b.** Shopping Online Takes Off
   - ☐ **c.** Art Students Everywhere

WRITING

A *Answer the questions in complete sentences based on your personal information.*

① Where do you go shopping?

_____

② How often do you go shopping?

_____

③ What do you usually buy when you go shopping?

_____

④ Do you spend a lot of money on clothes?

_____

⑤ Do you do online shopping? Why or why not?

_____

⑥ Do you think more people will do their shopping on the Internet in the future? Why or why not?

_____

B *Combine the following sentences based on the hints given.*

① { Daniel bought a pair of jeans.
    The pair of jeans is $350. (cost)

   The pair of jeans cost Daniel $350.

② { Cleaning our house took all day.
    We cleaned our house.

   It took _____

③ { My mother cooked a big meal.
    She spent an hour on it. (spend + V-ing)

   _____

④ { Sarah practiced the guitar yesterday.
    She spent three hours on it. (spend + V-ing)

   _____

⑤ { Jack spent a lot of money doing something.
    He bought computer games. (spend + on + N.)

   _____

CHALLENGE YOURSELF

Part I Pictures 🎧 2-27

Look at the picture and choose the best answer.

1.

☐ a   ☐ b   ☐ c

2.

☐ a   ☐ b   ☐ c

Part II Question & Response 🎧 2-28

Listen to the statement or question and choose the best response.

3. ☐ a   ☐ b   ☐ c   5. ☐ a   ☐ b   ☐ c
4. ☐ a   ☐ b   ☐ c   6. ☐ a   ☐ b   ☐ c

Part III Conversations 🎧 2-29

Listen to the conversation and answer the questions.

7. Why did he buy so many bags of dog food?
   ☐ a. To feed all of his dogs
   ☐ b. To get a better price
   ☐ c. To get a whole box

8. Why did Carson buy a purple sweater?
   ☐ a. Sweaters are in.
   ☐ b. He's very silly.
   ☐ c. Purple is in style.

9. What is true about the necklace?
   ☐ a. The man gave it to the woman.
   ☐ b. It cost the woman $1,000.
   ☐ c. The woman's husband gave it to her.

10. Why does Christine want to go to the flea market?
   ☐ a. She wants to buy some cheap stuff.
   ☐ b. She wants to get rid of some junk.
   ☐ c. She wants to see a boy she likes.

Linguaporta Training

Let's review the unit with Linguaporta.

UNIT
10

SHOP TILL YOU DROP

Going on Vacation

WARM UP

PICTURE DICTIONARY

Listen to the sentences. Each sentence is about something you need when traveling. Write the sentence number in the correct boxes below. CD 2-30

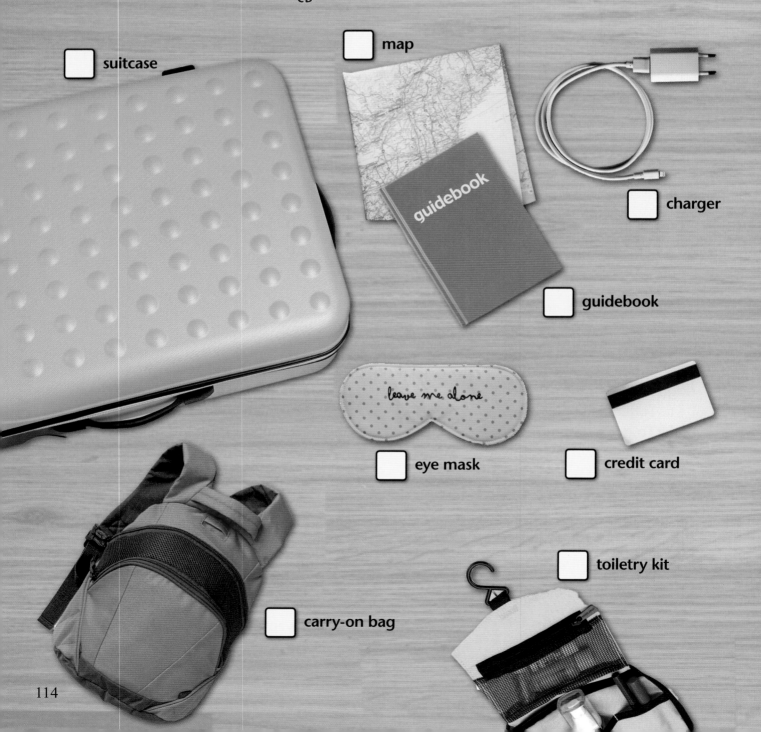

☐ suitcase

☐ map

☐ charger

☐ guidebook

☐ eye mask

☐ credit card

☐ toiletry kit

☐ carry-on bag

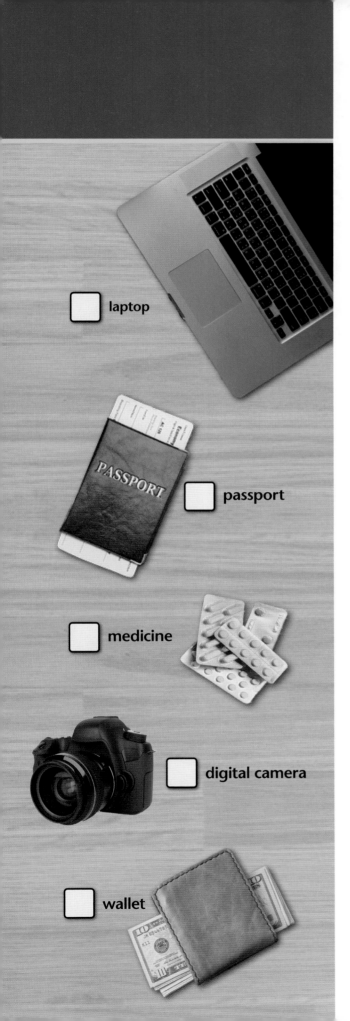

laptop

passport

medicine

digital camera

wallet

SET IN MOTION

A *Role-play with a partner. Use the vocabulary you have learned.*

   Ⓐ What should I bring on my trip?

   Ⓑ I think you should bring your _____.

   Ⓐ OK. Should I bring my _____, too?

   Ⓑ That would be a good idea.

B *Listen to the sentences again and fill in the blanks with words you have learned.*

1. I'll bring my _____ with me when I travel to the U.S., so I can contact you by e-mail.

2. Johnny keeps a picture of his daughter in his _____.

3. The store accepts _____.

4. Most people use the _____ on their smartphones to take pictures.

5. I always make sure my _____ is small enough to fit under my seat.

6. You will need to show your _____ to get into the country.

7. We looked at the _____ to find the bus station.

8. Most electrical mobile devices are sold with a _____ and travel case.

9. Before you visit a city, it's best to get a _____ so you can choose what to see.

10. Jack's _____ has a toothbrush, toothpaste, and shampoo.

11. I wore an _____ to help me fall asleep on the plane.

12. Michael packed some clothes in his _____.

13. The doctor gave me some _____ for my cold.

Making a Last-Minute Booking

A *Watch the video clip and check the correct answers.* 🖥️📱

1. What is the problem that Ray and Cathy encounter?
   - ☐ **a.** They realized they couldn't afford the trip.
   - ☐ **b.** They didn't make hotel reservations.
   - ☐ **c.** They couldn't find anywhere to stay.

2. What do we know about Ray and Cathy's flight to Italy?
   - ☐ **a.** It will occur in less than a week.
   - ☐ **b.** It was too expensive for their budget.
   - ☐ **c.** It will take off late at night.

3. What is true about Ray and Cathy's room in Italy?
   - ☐ **a.** It's small but cheap.
   - ☐ **b.** It's easily accessible by train.
   - ☐ **c.** It's in a bad location.

4. What is Ray likely going to do next?
   - ☐ **a.** Travel to Italy
   - ☐ **b.** Begin packing a suitcase
   - ☐ **c.** Keep looking for a rental apartment

I can't wait!

Italy, here we come!

B *Listen to the conversation and fill in the blanks.* 🎧 2-31 🖥️

Ray and Cathy's trip to Italy is approaching.

Ray: I still can't believe how cheap our fare was to Italy. I'm glad we ¹_____ our tickets.

Cathy: Italy, here we come! So, where are we staying anyway, Ray?

Ray: Umm ... didn't you mention that you were going to book the hotel?

Cathy: What? No, I thought you were going to do that.

Ray: Oh, man! We don't have ²_____ anywhere? We're going to have serious trouble finding a hotel room this late. The trip is in ³_____ than two days!

Cathy: Maybe if there's nothing ⁴_____, we can try finding a rental apartment.

Ray: Good thinking! I'll check those now. Let's see what we can find here.

Cathy: Well? Anything? I have a feeling most of the good rentals have probably been ⁵_____.

Ray: Well, let's see. Some of them are too expensive, but others are in bad locations. Wait! There's one remaining room available by Termini Station in Rome!

Cathy: Quick! Reserve it!

Ray: And ... OK! It's ⁶_____! It's going to be a little expensive for our budget, though.

Cathy: That's OK! We saved enough money on plane tickets. And it's ideal since it's so ⁷_____ to a train station. Anyway, I'm just glad we have a place to stay.

Ray: Me too! I'm so excited! I'm going to start ⁸_____ right now!

C *Practice the conversation with your partner.*

D *Listen to the two short conversations. What did the speaker book? Check the correct pictures.* 🎧 2-32

①

②

☐   ☐   ☐   ☐

one/both/some/most/all

 none/not any   any   some   most   all

Countable

Some Many Most Both All	+ of + N. + **V.** → *plural*

One Each (one) Every one None	+ of + N. + **V.** → *singular*

- <u>Some of the girls</u> in the classroom **were** sick.
- <u>Every one of my students</u> **has** a notebook.

Uncountable

All Most Some Part Half	+ of + N. + **V.** → *singular*

- <u>Half of the bread</u> **is** good.
- <u>Some of his art</u> **is** on display at the museum.

Work It Out

Ⓐ *Check the correct answers.*

① Half of the students (☐ participate / ☐ participates) in after-school clubs.

② One of the mountain climbers (☐ was / ☐ were) missing.

③ All of you (☐ has / ☐ have) to hand in a five-page report.

④ Most of the sidewalks in town (☐ is / ☐ are) made of bricks.

⑤ Some of the homework (☐ is / ☐ are) easy.

⑥ Both of my brothers (☐ is / ☐ are) teachers.

⑦ Most of the beef (☐ is / ☐ are) from Germany.

Ⓑ *Combine the sentences using **quantity pronouns**.*

① There are many flowers in the garden. All the flowers are pink.
All *of the flowers in the garden are pink.*

② Rita has many cousins here. Rita is going to visit a cousin here.
Rita _____

③ There are many students in the classroom. One student wears a red hat.
One _____

one ... the other ...

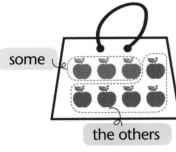

- I have two pens; **one** is long, and **the other** is short.

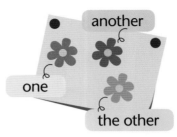

- There are three flowers; **one** is red, **another** is purple, and **the other** is pink.

some ... the others ...

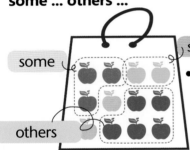

- **Some** apples are red, and **the others** are green.

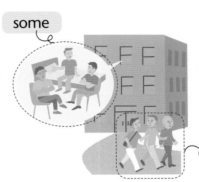

- **Some** people stayed in the dorm; **the others** went outside.

some ... others ...

- **Some** apples are red, **others** are green, and **still others** are yellow.

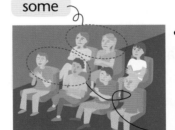

- **Some** thought the movie was boring, while **others** found it very funny.

UNIT
11

Work It Out

Ⓐ *Fill in the blanks.*

① Of the three friends, _____ wants to see a horror movie, _____ wants to see a sci-fi movie, and the other wants to see an action movie.

② There are three cars in the parking lot; one is black, and _____ are blue.

③ The two sisters are very different. _____ loves sports, and _____ likes music.

Ⓑ *Check the correct answers.*

① My brother has four kids. One of them (☐ is / ☐ are) a boy, and (☐ others / ☐ the others) are girls.

② Some of the children are six, and (☐ another / ☐ the others) are seven.

③ There are five pets in my house. Two are dogs and (☐ others / ☐ the others) are cats.

GOING ON VACATION

119

Italy's Beautiful Secret:
The Blue Grotto

2-33

You may have been to some famous places in Italy, such as Rome, Venice, and Sicily. However, there is another place in Italy that you should not miss. It is called Capri. Capri is a small island. Two thousand years ago, it was a resort for rich Romans. There are many fun and beautiful places in Capri.

5   Without a doubt, the Blue Grotto is a must-see. Almost everybody who visits Capri goes to the Blue Grotto. Its beauty is amazing. The Blue Grotto is a cave. To get there, you must take a boat. The entrance to the Blue Grotto is about one and a half meters wide. After you go through the
10   entrance, you'll be amazed. The water in the Blue Grotto is bright blue.

Some Romans believed that the grotto's water could cure sick people. Others believed that monsters lived in the grotto. If you visit the Blue Grotto, put your hand in the water. When you do this, your hand will turn blue, and it will glow!

A *Fill in the blanks with the word choices given. Change the word form if necessary.*

entrance / bright / cure / doubt / amazed

1. The lights are too _____. Turn them off.

2. I was _____ to hear that Mark had won first prize.

3. I'll meet you at the _____ to the park.

4. Will you be able to _____ my son, Doctor?

5. John is without _____ one of the finest swimmers in the school.

B *Check the correct answers.*

1. What is the Blue Grotto?
   - ☐ **a.** An island
   - ☐ **b.** A cave
   - ☐ **c.** A lake

2. How can you get to the Blue Grotto?
   - ☐ **a.** By boat
   - ☐ **b.** By plane
   - ☐ **c.** By train

3. How big is the entrance to the Blue Grotto?
   - ☐ **a.** About half a meter wide
   - ☐ **b.** About one meter wide
   - ☐ **c.** About one and a half meters wide

4. What color is the Blue Grotto?
   - ☐ **a.** Bright green
   - ☐ **b.** Bright blue
   - ☐ **c.** Dark blue

5. Which is NOT true?
   - ☐ **a.** Rome, Venice, and Sicily are located in Italy.
   - ☐ **b.** Capri was a resort for rich Romans.
   - ☐ **c.** You can see monsters in the grotto.

WRITING

A *Read the travel plan below. Make your own itinerary for one day of your dream vacation.*

DAY 1	December 13—NEW YORK CITY!
5:30–6:30 a.m.	**Wake up** Shower, get ready to leave hotel (*Make sure to bring backpack*)
6:30–7:30 a.m.	**Breakfast** Go to local bagel shop, buy newspaper from newsstand
7:30–8:00 a.m.	**Coffee shop** Try a local NYC coffee shop or diner
8:00–8:30 a.m.	**Taxi to bookstore** Experience a NYC taxi ride! (*Hopefully it's not too crazy*)
8:30–9:30 a.m.	**Strand Bookstore** Explore the legendary Strand Bookstore (*Find a rare book or two*)
9:45–11:30 a.m.	**Central Park!** Walk through Central Park, sit on a bench, take photos

DAY 3	(Date)—(Place)

B *Look at the pictures and complete the sentences.*

①  I have two books; _____

_____

②  There are three dogs; _____

_____

③  Jane has two brothers; _____

_____

122

CHALLENGE YOURSELF

Part I Pictures 🎵 2-34

Look at the picture and choose the best answer.

1.

☐ a   ☐ b   ☐ c

2.

☐ a   ☐ b   ☐ c

Part II Question & Response 🎵 2-35

Listen to the statement or question and choose the best response.

3. ☐ a   ☐ b   ☐ c   5. ☐ a   ☐ b   ☐ c
4. ☐ a   ☐ b   ☐ c   6. ☐ a   ☐ b   ☐ c

Part III Conversations 🎵 2-36

Listen to the conversation and answer the questions.

7. What does the woman say about her trip?
    ☐ a. She had a horrible time.
    ☐ b. She had a really good time.
    ☐ c. She didn't have time to go.

8. What does the woman want?
    ☐ a. To leave the hotel
    ☐ b. To get a room
    ☐ c. To have something to eat

9. What does the woman have to do?
    ☐ a. Call the hotel
    ☐ b. Put clothes in a bag
    ☐ c. Buy an airplane ticket

10. Where is the man?
    ☐ a. At a restaurant
    ☐ b. At a hotel
    ☐ c. At his house

Linguaporta Training

Let's review the unit with Linguaporta.

UNIT
11

GOING ON VACATION

123

WARM UP

PICTURE DICTIONARY

Listen to the sentences. Each sentence is about a different sport. Write the sentence number in the correct boxes below. CD 2-37

play basketball

play rugby

play soccer

jog / go jogging

swim / go swimming

play golf

play tennis

play baseball

play hockey

SET IN MOTION

A *Role-play with a partner. Use the vocabulary you have learned.*

Ⓐ What sport do you like?

Ⓑ I like _____.

Ⓐ How often do you _____?

Ⓑ _____.

....

Ⓐ Can you _____?

Ⓑ Yes, I can. / No, I can't.

B *Listen to the three conversations. Match the person with the sport that they like.* 🎧 2-38

go skating

Rick

play softball

Kathy

go skiing

Gary

☐ play volleyball

☐ do yoga

☐ work out

UNIT
12

SPORTS

125

What Sports Do You Like?

A *Watch the video clip and check the correct answers.* [WEB動画]

1. Why doesn't Bruce like baseball?
   - ☐ **a.** He thinks it is boring.
   - ☐ **b.** He thinks it is too hard.
   - ☐ **c.** He thinks it is too easy.

2. What sport does Ted like to watch?
   - ☐ **a.** Hockey
   - ☐ **b.** Baseball
   - ☐ **c.** Basketball

3. What does Bruce think of hockey?
   - ☐ **a.** It's very safe.
   - ☐ **b.** It's dangerous.
   - ☐ **c.** It's boring.

4. What sport does Bruce want to play with Ted?
   - ☐ **a.** Basketball
   - ☐ **b.** Hockey
   - ☐ **c.** Badminton

126

B *Listen to the conversation and fill in the blanks.* 2-39

Ted and Bruce are talking about their favorite sports.

Ted: I like baseball and basketball. What sports do you like, Bruce?

Bruce: I like basketball, but I don't like baseball. Baseball is slow and ¹_____.

Ted: Baseball isn't boring. I think it's exciting. I like ²_____ home runs!

Bruce: Oh, you like to play baseball. I like to play baseball, too. I just don't like ³_____ baseball.

Ted: I don't like to watch baseball, ⁴_____. I like to watch basketball.

Bruce: Me, too. Basketball is fun. Can you play basketball?

Ted: Yes, but I can't play basketball well. Basketball is ⁵_____.

Bruce: You're from Canada, right? So, do you like to watch hockey?

Ted: I LOVE to watch hockey. It's my favorite sport.

Bruce: Can you play hockey? I think hockey is ⁶_____.

Ted: Yes, I can play hockey, but I don't think it's dangerous.

Bruce: Why is hockey your favorite sport?

Ted: I like to play hockey because it's fast, and I love to ⁷_____!

Bruce: I still think it's dangerous. Come on, Ted. Let's play badminton. Badminton is ⁸_____!

C *Practice the conversation with your partner.*

D *Listen to the two conversations. What sports can the man or woman play? Write the conversation number in the correct boxes below.* 2-40

☐  ☐  ☐  ☐

Comparative Adjectives

$$A + be + \begin{cases} adj. \; \text{-er} \\ more + adj. \end{cases} + than + B$$

Bill is taller than Eason.

Superlative Adjectives

$$A + be + the + \begin{cases} adj. \; \text{-est} \\ most + adj. \end{cases}$$

Helen is the tallest of the three.

Regular

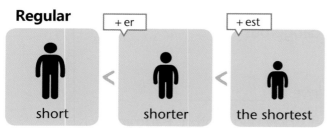

+ er   + est

short < shorter < the shortest

+ more   + the most

difficult < more difficult < the most difficult

Irregular

good < better < the best

bad < worse < the worst

$$A + be + less + adj. + than + B$$
$$= A + be + not + as + adj. + as + B$$

• This dog is less dangerous than you think.
  = This dog isn't as dangerous as you think.

$$adj.\text{-er} + than \begin{cases} \text{any other} \\ \text{all the other} \\ \text{anything/anyone else} \end{cases}$$

• The giraffe is the tallest animal in the world.
  = The giraffe is taller than any other animal in the world.
  = The giraffe is taller than all the other animals in the world.
  = No other animal in the world is as tall as the giraffe.
  = No other animal in the world is taller than the giraffe.

I'm the tallest!

Work It Out

A *Check the correct answers.*

① The girl is really (☐ cute / ☐ cuter / ☐ cutest).

② She's the (☐ old / ☐ older / ☐ oldest) child in her family.

③ I'm (☐ tall / ☐ taller / ☐ tallest) than my father.

④ Rita is the (☐ good / ☐ better / ☐ best) student in the class.

⑤ It was the (☐ difficult / ☐ more difficult / ☐ most difficult) test I've ever taken.

B *Fill in the blanks based on the hints given.*

① A: Who is the boy over there?

B: He's my brother.

A: You're much _____ (tall) _____ him.

B: Yes, I'm three years _____ (old) than him.

A: No wonder!

② A: What do you think of English? Is it _____ (easy) _____ math?

B: Of course. I think math is the _____ (difficult) subject for me.

A: And the _____ (boring) subject, too.

C *Rewrite the sentences based on the hints given.*

① Anna is the kindest of all the people I've ever met.

= Anna is _kinder than any other person I've ever met._ (any other)

= Anna is _____ (all the other)

= Anna is _____ (anyone else)

= No other _____ (as … as)

② The blue shoes are less expensive than the pink shoes.

= The blue shoes _____ (as … as)

③ Michelle is the most popular student in class.

= No other _____ (adj.-er than / more
+ adj. than)

Challenge Yourself in the Ironman Triathlon

2-41

3.86KM

180.25KM

42.2KM

The Ironman Triathlon is the hardest race in the world. Only the best athletes can finish it. To start the Ironman Triathlon, first you swim 3.86 kilometers. After that, you ride a bike 180.25 kilometers. Finally, you have to run 42.2 kilometers. During the race, you cannot
5 take a break. You must finish the race in less than 17 hours. Do you know why we call this race the Ironman Triathlon? People say that if you finish this race, you are an "ironman" or an "ironwoman." Your body is as strong as iron.

Before people join the Ironman Triathlon, they train for a long
10 time. People do other things to prepare. They eat healthy food every day. They also study the Ironman Triathlon. Some professional athletes want to win the Ironman Triathlon. However, most people don't care about that. They just want to finish the race. They want to challenge themselves.

A *Fill in the blanks with the word choices given. Change the word form if necessary.*

> athlete / prepare / professional / healthy / challenge

1. Many people today are adopting a _____ lifestyle.
2. Jenny began her _____ career as a dancer 10 years ago.
3. Can I _____ you to a game of tennis?
4. Ted was busy _____ to go on holiday.
5. Luke is one of the greatest _____ of all time.

B *Check the correct answers.*

1. What is the first part of the Ironman Triathlon?
   - ☐ **a.** The running race
   - ☐ **b.** The bike race
   - ☐ **c.** The swim

2. What is the longest part of the Ironman Triathlon?
   - ☐ **a.** The running race
   - ☐ **b.** The bike race
   - ☐ **c.** The swim

3. Which is true about the Ironman Triathlon?
   - ☐ **a.** You can take a break during the race.
   - ☐ **b.** It's the toughest race in the world.
   - ☐ **c.** You cannot finish the race in less than 17 hours.

4. Why do people call this race the Ironman Triathlon?
   - ☐ **a.** Your body is strong like iron if you finish this race.
   - ☐ **b.** Your body is as hard as iron if you finish this race.
   - ☐ **c.** You're a superhero like Iron Man if you finish this race.

5. What is another suitable title for this article?
   - ☐ **a.** The History of the Ironman Triathlon
   - ☐ **b.** How to Win the Ironman Triathlon
   - ☐ **c.** The Hardest Race in the World

UNIT
12

SPORTS

A *Complete the sentences using superlative adjectives (the ... in the world). Then, rewrite the sentence based on the hints given.*

① Angel Falls, high, waterfall

Angel Falls is the highest waterfall in the world.

= Angel Falls is higher than any other waterfall. _____ (than any other)

② The Great Wall of China, long, wall

_____

= _____ (than any other)

③ Mt. Everest, high, mountain

_____

= _____ (than anything else)

④ The Pacific Ocean, large, ocean

_____

= _____ (No other ... as adj. as)

B *Answer the following questions. Then, write a paragraph based on your answers.*

• Favorite sport: _____

• ☐ I like to play _____ (sport).

  ☐ I can't play _____ (sport).

  I just like to watch it.

• Why you like _____ (favorite sport):

_____

_____

_____

CHALLENGE YOURSELF

Look at the picture and choose the best answer.

1.

   ☐ a   ☐ b   ☐ c

2.

   ☐ a   ☐ b   ☐ c

Part II **Question & Response** 🎧 2-43

Listen to the statement or question and choose the best response.

3. ☐ a   ☐ b   ☐ c   5. ☐ a   ☐ b   ☐ c
4. ☐ a   ☐ b   ☐ c   6. ☐ a   ☐ b   ☐ c

Part III **Conversations** 🎧 2-44

Listen to the conversation and answer the questions.

7. Which sentence is true?
   ☐ a. Both Jeff and Jane play hockey well.
   ☐ b. Maybe they'll practice tennis together.
   ☐ c. Jeff is able to skate better than Jane.

8. Why does he like the Oakland A's?
   ☐ a. They're the most popular team in the world.
   ☐ b. They play together like a united team.
   ☐ c. He's from the same city as the baseball team.

9. How does Anne feel about most sports?
   ☐ a. She only likes to play summer sports.
   ☐ b. She thinks all sports are boring.
   ☐ c. They make her feel uncomfortable.

10. What does the woman like to do?
    ☐ a. Watch baseball
    ☐ b. Play baseball
    ☐ c. Play basketball

UNIT
12

SPORTS

Linguaporta Training

Let's review the unit with Linguaporta.

Part I 🎧 2-45

Listen to the statement or question and check the best response.

1. ☐ a ☐ b ☐ c
2. ☐ a ☐ b ☐ c
3. ☐ a ☐ b ☐ c
4. ☐ a ☐ b ☐ c

Part II 🎧 2-46

Listen to the conversation and check the correct answer.

1. What does the woman think about the shirt?
   - ☐ a. She thinks it's expensive.
   - ☐ b. She thinks it's reasonable.
   - ☐ c. She thinks it's very cheap.

2. What is the woman going to do on Sunday?
   - ☐ a. Hike in the mountain
   - ☐ b. Play video games
   - ☐ c. Ride a bike

3. What will the woman cook tonight?
   - ☐ a. Beef
   - ☐ b. Fish
   - ☐ c. Chicken

4. What does the woman say about Austria?
   - ☐ a. It has beautiful buildings, towns, and cities.
   - ☐ b. It has beautiful mountains, rivers, and forests.
   - ☐ c. It has beautiful people and delicious food.

Part III 🎧 2-47

Listen to the short passage and check the correct picture.

1.

 ☐ a
 ☐ b
 ☐ c

2.

 ☐ a
 ☐ b
 ☐ c

Part IV

Fill in the blanks.

> check / pack / customers / million / insects / discount / island / menu / climb / makes a living

1. Desserts are on the last page of the _____.
2. The huge house costs more than one _____ dollars.
3. Many kids like to _____ trees.
4. Please _____ this sentence for me.
5. Lucy _____ as an interior designer.
6. That café is always packed with _____.
7. We went to a quiet _____ on our vacation.
8. Did you _____ enough clothes for the trip?
9. There's a 10 percent _____ on all clothes on this rack.
10. Mosquitoes and flies are _____.

Part V

Check the correct answer.

1. You should _____ less time surfing the Internet.
   ☐ **a.** cost ☐ **b.** take ☐ **c.** pay ☐ **d.** spend

2. How _____ did these shoes cost you?
   ☐ **a.** much ☐ **b.** long ☐ **c.** many ☐ **d.** often

3. I got two gifts. One is a watch, and _____ is a purse.
   ☐ **a.** other ☐ **b.** others ☐ **c.** the other ☐ **d.** the others

4. Judy is much _____ than the other girls at school.
   ☐ **a.** pretty ☐ **b.** more pretty ☐ **c.** prettier ☐ **d.** prettiest

5. The book you're holding is _____.
   ☐ **a.** I ☐ **b.** my ☐ **c.** me ☐ **d.** mine

6. My credit card _____ while I was shopping.
   ☐ **a.** stole ☐ **b.** was stolen ☐ **c.** stolen ☐ **d.** was stealing

7. I'm sorry I was late. It _____ happen again.
   ☐ **a.** won't ☐ **b.** will ☐ **c.** is going ☐ **d.** is not going

8. This coffee _____ medicine.
   ☐ **a.** taste ☐ **b.** tastes ☐ **c.** tastes like ☐ **d.** tasted

9. Do you want to buy _____ beverages?
   ☐ **a.** much ☐ **b.** any ☐ **c.** little ☐ **d.** a little

10. Peter is the _____ all the players.
    ☐ **a.** taller in ☐ **b.** taller of ☐ **c.** tallest in ☐ **d.** tallest of

Read the article and check the correct answer.

Don't Judge an Animal by Its Looks

"Look at that chimpanzee! Isn't that cute?"

"Wow! I bet that shark is dangerous."

We often think cute animals are sweet and scary animals are super dangerous. However, we should <u>never judge a book by its cover</u>. Many cute animals are very dangerous. Other animals
5 are less dangerous than you think. Take sharks, for example. They look terrifying—and they're dangerous, of course—but they seldom attack people. On the other hand, chimpanzees are cute, funny, and smart. That doesn't matter! Chimpanzees are also dangerous, and they often attack people.

Many people hate spiders. They can run fast and they have long,
10 ugly legs. That doesn't mean you should always fear them. Some spiders have poison, but most are harmless. How about hippos? They're fat, and they look silly. Therefore, they're not dangerous, right? Wrong! Hippos kill people all the time. In fact, they're one of Africa's most dangerous animals. Sometimes, the smallest creatures are the most dangerous ones by far.
15 Mosquitoes are very dangerous, because sometimes they make people sick. Every year, mosquitoes give diseases to millions of people.

1. What can we say about sharks?
   - [ ] **a.** They attack people all the time.
   - [ ] **b.** They are afraid of people.
   - [ ] **c.** They don't often attack people.

2. What does the underlined phrase "never judge a book by its cover" mean?
   - [ ] **a.** Don't make decisions without thinking twice.
   - [ ] **b.** Don't base your opinion of something on the way it looks.
   - [ ] **c.** Don't take something or someone for granted.

3. According to the article, what can we say about chimpanzees?
   - [ ] **a.** They look cute, but they're dangerous.
   - [ ] **b.** They aren't dangerous and seldom attack people.
   - [ ] **c.** They look scary and often attack people.

4. How many spiders are dangerous?

☐ **a.** All of them

☐ **b.** Just a few of them

☐ **c.** None of them

5. Which sentence is true?

☐ **a.** Sharks are as dangerous as you think.

☐ **b.** Hippos are one of the world's most dangerous animals.

☐ **c.** Mosquitoes are less dangerous than spiders.

Part VII

Fill in the blanks and answer the questions in complete sentences with the hints given.

1. _____ people are there in your family? *(five)*

_____

2. _____ do you like, noodles or rice? *(rice)*

_____

3. _____ is going with you? *(Mike and Sarah)*

_____

4. _____ does it feel? *(cotton)*

_____

5. _____ do you look so tired? *(study all night)*

_____

Answer the questions in complete sentences based on your personal information.

1. Are you good at speaking in front of a lot of people?

_____

2. Do you post a lot of photos on social media?

_____

3. Do you have a part-time job?

_____

4. What are you going to do this weekend?

_____

5. Do you like shopping? How often do you go shopping?

_____

リンガポルタのご案内

LINGUAPORTA

リンガポルタ連動テキストをご購入の学生さんは、「リンガポルタ」を無料でご利用いただけます！

本テキストで学習していただく内容に準拠した問題を、オンライン学習システム「リンガポルタ」で学習していただくことができます。PCだけでなく、スマートフォンやタブレットでも学習できます。単語や文法、リスニング力などをよりしっかり身に付けていただくため、ぜひ積極的に活用してください。

リンガポルタの利用にはアカウントとアクセスコードの登録が必要です。登録方法については下記ページにアクセスしてください。

https://www.seibido.co.jp/linguaporta/register.html

本テキスト「Live Escalate Book 1: Base Camp」のアクセスコードは下記です。

7221-2045-1231-0365-0003-0069-CK3G-R2NE

・リンガポルタの学習機能（画像はサンプルです。また、すべてのテキストに以下の4つの機能が用意されているわけではありません）

多肢選択

空所補充（音声を使っての聞き取り問題も可能）

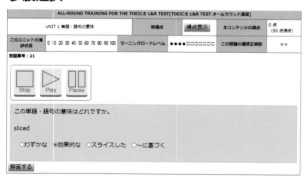

単語並びかえ（マウスや手で単語を移動）

マッチング（マウスや手で単語を移動）

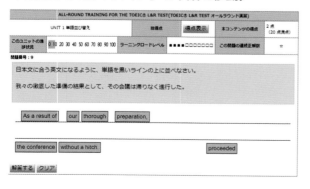

Web動画のご案内　$\mathcal{S}$StreamLine

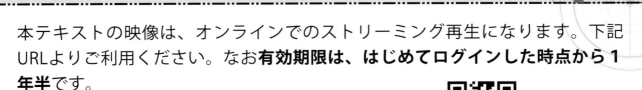

本テキストの映像は、オンラインでのストリーミング再生になります。下記URLよりご利用ください。なお**有効期限は、はじめてログインした時点から1年半**です。

http://st.seibido.co.jp

① ログイン画面

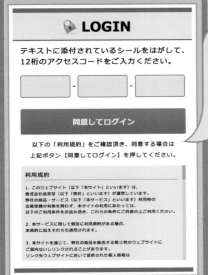

巻末に添付されているシールをはがして、アクセスコードをご入力ください。

② メニュー画面

「Video」または「Audio」を選択すると、それぞれストリーミング再生ができます。

③ 再生画面

推奨動作環境

【PC OS】
Windows 7~　/　Mac 10.8~

【Mobile OS】
iOS / Android ※Android の場合は4.x~が推奨

【Desktop ブラウザ】
Internet Explorer 9~ / Firefox / Chrome / Safari / Microsoft Edge

TEXT PRODUCTION STAFF

edited by	編集
Takashi Kudo	工藤 隆志

cover design by	表紙デザイン
Nobuyoshi Fujino	藤野 伸芳

text design by	本文デザイン
Ruben Frosali	ルーベン・フロサリ

CD PRODUCTION STAFF

recorded by	吹き込み者
Rachel Walzer (AmE)	レイチェル・ワルザー (アメリカ英語)
Howard Colefield (AmE)	ハワード・コールフィルド (アメリカ英語)
Dominic Allen (AmE)	ドミニク・アレン (アメリカ英語)
Karen Haedrich (AmE)	カレン・ヘドリック (アメリカ英語)

Live Escalate Book 1: Base Camp

2021年1月10日　初版発行
2024年2月25日　第5刷発行

著　　者	角山 照彦
	Live ABC editors
発 行 者	佐野 英一郎
発 行 所	株式会社 成美堂
	〒101-0052　東京都千代田区神田小川町3-22
	TEL 03-3291-2261　FAX 03-3293-5490
	https://www.seibido.co.jp

印刷・製本　(株)加藤文明社

ISBN 978-4-7919-7221-0　　　　　　　　　　Printed in Japan